T0281858

BACK TO ISTANBUL

BACK TO ISTANBUL

ON FOOT ACROSS EUROPE TO THE GREAT SILK ROAD

BERNARD OLLIVIER & BÉNÉDICTE FLATET

TRANSLATED BY DAN GOLEMBESKI

Skyhorse Publishing

To Henri

OTHER BOOKS BY THE SAME AUTHOR AVAILABLE IN ENGLISH

Out of Istanbul: A Journey of Discovery along the Silk Road. Skyhorse Publishing, 2019.

Walking to Samarkand: The Great Silk Road from Persia to Central Asia. Skyhorse Publishing, 2020.

Winds of the Steppe: Walking the Great Silk Road from Central Asia to China. Skyhorse Publishing, 2020.

CONTENTS

Prologue: One More Adventure?   XI

PART ONE: LYON TO VERONA   1

    I.   The Canuts   3

   II.   First Border   12

  III.   Our Italian Campaign   19

  IV.   The Naviglio Grande   25

    V.   Solferino: The Bloody Hill   29

PART TWO: VERONA TO ISTANBUL   39

  Through Bénédicte's Eyes   41

  Setting Out—July 29, 2014   43

  VI.   Exhaustion   44

 VII.   Venice and Trieste   52

  Trieste—August 14   63

VIII.   The Mountains   64

  IX.   Croatia: The Crocodile's Jaw   67

  Jajce, Central Bosnia—September 2   84

   X.   Landmines Ahead!   87

  XI.   The Balkans: After the Hatred   95

 XII.   Sarajevo Roses   103

XIII.	Tunnels	110
	Goražde—September 12	123
XIV.	Montenegro	127
XV.	A Serbian Hiatus	131
XVI.	Kosovo: The Dividing Line Between Coffee and Tea	135
XVII.	Macedonia	143
	Skopje, Macedonia—September 21: Our 8th Border Crossing	149
XVIII.	Bulgaria	152
	Plovdiv, Bulgaria—October 2	158
	Harmanli, Bulgaria—October 5	169
XIX.	Adrianople—Edirne	181
	Lüleburgaz, Turkey—October 13	185
XX.	Drawing Near	188
XXI.	Back to Istanbul	193
	Çorlu, Turkey—October 14: T-Minus Four Days	195
	Istanbul!—October 17	200
	Back Home—October 24	204
Epilogue: The Balkans: Corridor Between Life and Death		207
Acknowledgments		209
About the Authors		211
Translator's Afterword: Walking as a Way of Life		215

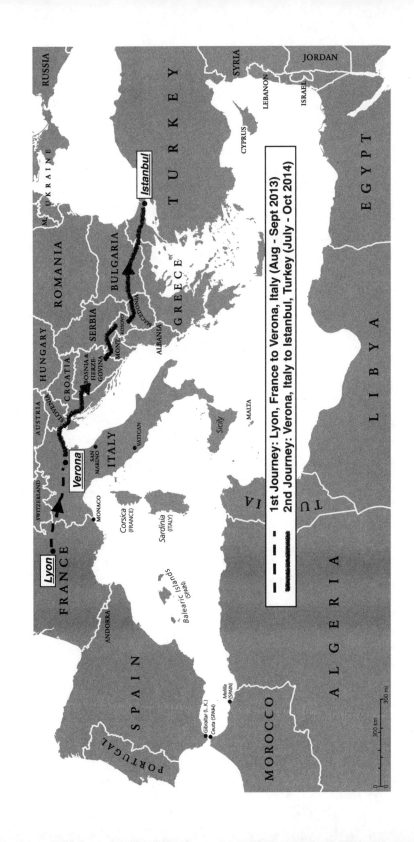

1st Journey: Lyon, France to Verona, Italy (Aug - Sept 2013)
2nd Journey: Verona, Italy to Istanbul, Turkey (July - Oct 2014)

PROLOGUE
ONE MORE ADVENTURE?

As we cross over into the autumn of our lives, we must at some point wonder when to call it quits. To quit everything: travel, walking, meeting people—to cease dreaming of all we'd like to do in the world. For how long can we laugh off the ticking clock? Up to what age can we rely on our bodies? When do we accept what some would call "being reasonable" and others "giving up"? I've asked myself these questions many times after one unforgettable day in the spring of 2012.

Bénédicte and I were finishing our lunch out on the veranda, enjoying its view of the wild cherry trees I planted, which were in full bloom. When the topic of conversation turned to walking, Bénédicte suddenly asked: "Why—when you decided to travel the Silk Road—didn't you leave from France, the way you did when you set out for Compostela?"

"What are you suggesting? That a 7,500-mile hike wasn't enough? That I should have added 1,900 more between France and Istanbul and dodge bullets in Kosovo?" I replied ironically. I then pointed out that, as far as I was concerned, the Great Silk Road was first and foremost in Asia.

But on second thought, I added: "You're right, though: I could very well have set out from Lyon. After all, in the late nineteenth century, it was the greatest silk-making city in the world. It's true that the Silk Road really did begin—or end, rather—right here at home."

At that, my companion raised her eyes to the sky and struck a pose of deep reflection.

"So why don't you complete what you started by walking from Lyon to Istanbul?"

I laughed.

"*Ma chérie*, I'm seventy-five. I'm an old man! When I finally set foot in Xi'an in 2002, I was in the best shape of my life. But that was ten years ago!"

"What an amazing journey it would be! And you know what would make it even more marvelous? If I went with you."

We sipped coffee and spoke of something else. But the seed had been planted. Instead of immediately lying down for an after-lunch siesta, I spread a large map of Europe out on a table and pored over the route I might have taken: the Alps, Italy, the Balkans, and at last the part of Turkey that sits in Europe. A thousand images came rushing back to me: the landscapes, the faces, the deserts crossed, the occasional fears, the countless joys, the unforgettable encounters, and much much more. All hopes of a nap crumbled.

Little by little, a silken dream wove its way into my mind: I envisioned merchants in Lyon unloading large bundles of silkworms from the Far East, Central Asia, and the Balkans; the clickity-clack of the weaving shuttles resounded in my ears; I pictured myself crossing borders. I was soon hooked, my head spinning with all that such a journey would surely bring—the stories, the encounters, the delightful moments of fatigue.

But how am I to ignore all the pains old age has plagued me with? Poor circulation, kidney stones, a slightly enlarged prostate, a faltering memory. Not to mention—and this should amuse those who take me for a natural athlete—my flat feet! Then there's the carotid artery stenosis discovered only a few weeks ago: a little fatty build-up, which, were it to detach, might easily lead to a stroke, either killing or partially paralyzing me. It's a kind of biological hand grenade and the pin has already been pulled out. No, too much time has passed! Ten years ago: why not? But today, even with the little walk or jog I do each morning, followed by some stretching, I see that, day by day and year by year, time is imperceptibly, ruthlessly whittling down my strength, chipping away at it. It's time for me to permanently put away my hiking boots and pull out my slippers. I ought to plop myself down on the couch and buy myself one of those big flat-screen TVs that decorate the living room of every self-respecting retiree. I'm at that age when you say: "I've done my part, let others now pick up where I left off."

Still, the little seed Bénédicte had planted kept right on growing. At what age must we accept dying? I, for one, am not yet ready. For the past fifteen years, retirement has kept me constantly busy. Establishing the Seuil Association to help troubled teens get back on track through long, therapeutic walks,* and writing some twelve books in thirteen years—as a "retiree," I've never lacked for work.

But why another walk? Good question. But here's another: Why not? Why claim a need for rest when each day draws me a little nearer to *eternal repose*?

I unfold the map of Europe: the Balkans are both near . . . and far. Some have populations smaller than a single French region. On paper, they're so interlocked they resemble a jigsaw puzzle. And what does the word "border" even mean in these regions where, for two millennia, history, religion, and war piled one wave of migration upon another, creating a gigantic demographic millefeuille pastry? What jumps out at me from my unfolded map is the existence of three distinct Europes. First, Western Europe, comprised of prosperous countries, despite cyclical crises. Second, the Europe of the former Soviet buffer zone, from Estonia to Romania, whose economies are on the upswing. And finally, a third Europe, which can be summed up as the former patchwork-State of Yugoslavia. A Europe still on life support and licking its wounds. Tito had unified these dissimilar countries, whose cultures and religions conflict. Famous for having resisted first the Nazis, then the Soviet ogre that sought

---

* Website: assoseuil.org. See description at the end of this volume.

to devour him, he managed to maintain a facade of unity. Ten years after his death in 1981, the region literally imploded.

War, the horrors of "ethnic cleansing," the sieges of Sarajevo and Goražde, the massacre of Srebrenica—it all made headlines for a time, but then silence returned, that of the cemeteries. The resulting wounds have, it seems, been bandaged. But did anyone succeed in reducing the fever? Nothing could be less certain, especially since war is now thundering just beyond the European Union's borders. Ukraine, Syria, Iraq, Afghanistan, Libya: the violence seems to never let up; death is on the prowl. It's true that, along the Great Silk Road, up and down the former caravan routes, peace never prevailed: there were wars of conquest, guerilla skirmishes, and revolutions—one Russian, one Chinese, and one Islamic in Iran. There was bloodshed in Afghanistan as I started my journey out of Istanbul. Local conflicts continued unabated between the Turks and the Kurds, the Uyghurs and the Chinese. For my own safety, I had to skirt around Tajikistan. In Kosovo, people have put down their weapons, but for how long?

"By traveling those 1,900 miles from Lyon to Istanbul," the mischief-maker within me whispered, "you'll see for yourself the state of this eastern Europe, which people hardly ever even mention anymore. How well are the region's Muslims and Christians—both Orthodox and Catholic—getting along today after having experienced the worst possible hatred of all, the kind that's directed at one's own neighbors and cousins? How are the martyred cities recovering? What has become of the mafias, the minefields, and the various forms of trafficking? Is fear now gone for good? Has trust been restored to these men and women, torn between armies ready to kill in the name of their own particular God . . . and their own interests?" These were but a few of the questions running through my mind.

With leaving a foregone conclusion now that I was itching to walk again, the question remained: should Bénédicte and I travel together, as she had suggested? I've always walked alone. Despite plenty of invitations, I never once gave up my right to wend my way in the solitude that suits me so well. Hiking makes me happy, accompanied by the sound of my boots on the sand or asphalt, birdsong from above, the patter of a surprised animal darting out in front of me, or even the roar of passing trucks. Walking is thinking. No words must break the thread of reflection. As I walk, I move toward the world and the world moves toward me. There's nothing like a healthy dose of solitude out on the trail to turn a quiet fellow into a chatterbox the moment another human being comes into view. Differences of culture, history, or language fall away. Communication takes place through the hands, the eyes, the heart.

I've walked some three hundred miles with Bénédicte. In Normandy, Portugal, the Pyrenees, Turkey, and—before the bullets began to fly—in Syria. My partner is a very good walker, and she, too, appreciates silence. Still, having faced life-threatening situations on my long Silk Road journey, I'm well aware of the dangers that come with this kind of adventure. To some, all Europeans' pockets are lined with gold, and there are plenty of mafiosos out there who'd be more than happy to help them lighten their load. And what's more: respect for the fairer sex is not the most widespread virtue in these parts. Am I ready to take the risks? For myself, yes, of course. But what about for her?

Still, why would I keep Bénédicte from realizing her dream? She's strong; difficult weather never puts her off. And it so happens that, when we met for the first time, we noticed yet another trait we had in common, one that delights us: we're equally tall and walk at the same pace. "When, for the first time, we went strolling along the banks of the Seine and I noticed how we were walking at precisely the same speed, I slipped my hand in yours for I knew at that very moment you were the man I'd been waiting for," she told me one day.

Alright then. Let's hit the road!

We will need at least four months to cover the almost 1,900 miles that separate Lyon from Istanbul. I keep a busy schedule, and so does Bénédicte. Twisting our calendars in every imaginable way, we decided to split the journey in two: one month straddling August and September 2013, then three months the following year. With, sadly, an obligatory second violation of my core principles: we'll carry a cellphone with us, since, for her job, Bénédicte has to stay "connected," whereas I, for my part, have grown mildly addicted to email.

In 2013, we'll travel from Lyon to Verona, and in 2014, from Verona to Istanbul. The first leg comprises about 560 miles; the second, just over 1,240. The route includes a dozen border crossings. All we had left to do was zip up our packs and hit the trail. It's a bit like our honeymoon too, since, after living together for several years, in March 2013, we decided to get "PACSed", which provided a happy pretext for us to invite all our friends over for a feel-good get-together before our grand departure.*

All things considered, I was delighted to finally be wrapping up my "*longue marche*," begun in Istanbul and completed in Xi'an. Bénédicte had been right to question me: a section had been missing from my Great Silk Road journey. And today we embark on its next—and final—leg.

---

* TN (Translator's Note): The PACS is France's 1999 "*pacte civil de solidarité.*" To get "*PACSé*" is to enter into a civil union. The PACS allows any two adults to legally organize their lives together.

BACK TO ISTANBUL

PART ONE:
LYON TO VERONA

I

THE CANUTS

August 20, 2013. Bénédicte is ecstatic to be heading to the Orient with the one man she considers a bona fide adventurer. As for me, nothing has changed. It may well be that leaving is "to die a little," but above all, it means stressing out. Every time I set out on a walk it was several days into the journey before the stress finally let up. At Lyon-Perrache train station, with our packs on our backs, we lug a heavy duffel bag. Carefully folded up inside is Ulysses, my pull-cart companion who accompanied me from Samarkand, Uzbekistan to Xi'an, China.

The tour we take of "La Maison des Canuts"—The Silk Workers' Center—is a tad disappointing for the specialist I've become, but I'm sure that the other tourists in our group find it fascinating. Our guide spins the history of silk for us, leaving nothing, or nearly nothing, out. Least of all the legend of the princess who accidentally dropped a cocoon she was playing with into her cup of steaming tea, only to pull out a thread a kilometer long. A royal discovery.

And a royal privilege: wearing the precious fabric was a right reserved for the Emperor of China and his family. The penalty for anyone caught transporting the secret outside the Middle Kingdom was death. For two thousand years it was a secret safely kept until it was finally revealed to the Occident by three monks who, as the story goes, smuggled out cocoons hidden inside their hollowed-out walking sticks. Another legend claims that a Chinese princess, married against her will to a Kazakh sheep farmer and fearing that she would find herself having to wear coarse wool, snuck a few cocoons out in her chignon. The true story is less romantic. When the Chinese attempted to invade modern-day Kyrgyzstan, at the Battle of Talas, in 751, three thousand soldiers from the Middle Kingdom were taken prisoner and sent to Damascus and Baghdad. These warriors, former artisans but henceforth slaves, set about making, on one hand, paper—which, used in printing, would lead to the greatest technological revolution of all time—and on the other, silk.

And so, the Near East acquired the secret of the *Bombyx*, that curious furry moth from whose eggs emerge tiny larvae. They gorge themselves on mulberry leaves, then, in preparation for molting, wrap themselves in a fine thread until it forms a shell. From Damascus to Constantinople, from Italy to eventually France, silk-making would become a thriving industry.

Francis I, monarch from 1515 to 1547, finding it a bit excessive to allow four to five hundred thousand gold *écus* to leave France for the purchase of silk goods in Italy, granted silk-making privileges to the city of Lyon. Stefan Turchetti, an Italian importer, was the first to produce silk fabric in the city, having lured over a number of Italian silk makers, our first and most welcome immigrant workers. The city owes its fortunes to them. The precious fabric was first used to dress the Prelates of the Papal Court. In 1541, there were forty looms in the city. By 1548, that number had grown to over a thousand, along with 459 master weavers. Two years later, 12,000 individuals were earning a living from silk-making. Henry IV had 60,000 mulberry trees planted in France, including 20,000 in Paris's Tuileries Gardens. By 1660, Lyon boasted 3,000 master weavers and 10,000 looms. The Revocation of the Edict of Nantes in 1685 and the ensuing flight of Protestants from the country drove the number of looms down to 4,000; the French Revolution further reduced their number to 2,000. But the First and Second Empires led to the city's fabulous revival. By the time Napoleon Bonaparte was crowned emperor in 1804, the number of looms was back to 10,000. Their number grew to 30,000 in 1830, 60,000 in 1848, and 120,000 in 1877. Switzerland, Prussia, Saxony, and, above all, England had silk industries of their own. During this period, Lyon became Europe's capital of fashion, thanks to the creation of a school of talented couturiers whose designs took every court on the continent by storm.

Our tour guide mentions nothing, however, of the Canut Revolts: how small owners and factory workers rose up on several occasions against their bosses to defend their rights. Clashes in 1831 resulted in some 600 deaths. The Canuts brandished a flag that, in gold letters on a velvet background, proclaimed: *VIVRE EN TRAVAILLANT OU MOURIR EN COMBATTANT* (LIVE WORKING OR DIE FIGHTING). In 1894, Aristide Bruant's hit song *"C'est nous, les Canuts, nous sommes tout nus,"* popularized what is considered France's first major working-class uprising.[*]

Today, little remains of Lyon's silk saga. The invention of the Jacquard loom, more efficient than earlier manual versions, reduced the need for manpower and threw many Canuts out of work. Then came the silkworm plague. Finally, the invention of rayon—a.k.a. "poor man's silk"—was the final blow. Nowadays, China has regained its status as the world's largest silk producer. Here in France, we've shut down the magnaneries[†] and pulled out mulberry bushes in order to plant grapes. Among the Canuts who lost their jobs, one by the name of Laurent Mourguet was destined to become rather famous.[‡] He loved telling stories, so he created Lyon's most famous ambassador: the puppet Guignol and his accomplice Gnafron. He made him rebellious and outspoken, a voice for the humiliated and unemployed like himself, for all those whom life had robbed, or who had been

---

[*] TN: "We, the Canuts, have nothing to wear." From the *Chant des Canuts*, written by Aristide Bruant in 1894. This song of revolt was later recorded by many French singers, such as Yves Montand, and is still cited today by politicians whenever they seek to defend workers' interests.
[†] TN: Silk-making factories.
[‡] TN: Laurent Mourguet, 1769–1844.

robbed of their lives. And he exacts a little payback: Guignol's the one who wields the stick and it's the gendarmes who get whacked.

On the morning of August 21, we part ways with Michelle and Georges, our marvelous hosts, and exit Lyon by way of the aptly named *"Porte des Alpes."* I take Ulysses out of his bag and reassemble him. We've carried him this far: it's now his turn to carry our bags all the way to Istanbul. These are our first days out walking, and they lead us down narrow roads lined with flower gardens behind which stand graceless detached houses, many with closed shutters since their owners are on vacation. Shopkeepers have also left in search of sun and idle pleasures. Very few people return our boom-ing *"Bonjours!"* We draw only silent stares. One can never be too careful when it comes to nomads, and our offbeat buggy is cause for suspicion. Victor Hugo makes a reference to wanderers in *The Man Who Laughs*, saying that every "passer-by was a possible public enemy."* In Asia, I was day in and day out in contact with rural pop-ulations unlike me in every possible way: language, culture, religion, and more. But everywhere I went, I was greeted with wonderful hos-pitality and immense curiosity. This is an altogether different world. French countryfolk of yesteryear, isolated in their home regions, were hospitable to those passing through. But they've been replaced by bedroom-community city folk who work downtown and return to the countryside for its peace and quiet only. They're uninterested in village life. These days in France, in order to speak to a foreigner, someone has to introduce you first.

    The only hotel in the village of La Verpillière is closed. So we do a little *camping sauvage* beside a marsh drainage ditch, where we're divebombed by mosquitoes. Except in the desert, I hate camp-ing. I know going into it how I'll suffer from the lack of comfort,

---

* TN: *L'homme qui rit*, Paris: Nelson, Éditeurs, 1869. Quotation from *The Man Who Laughs*, The Kelmscott Society Publishers, New York, translated by Isabel F. Hapgood, 1888, T. Y. Crowell & Co., 42.

from wetness, and from stones discovered only *after* the tent has been pitched. Bénédicte, on the other hand, absolutely loves it. In the morning, two highway police officers come bouncing down a grassy path astride powerful motorcycles. Given the conditions, they advance at a crawl. They're trying to find a motorcyclist who, a short while ago, forced his way through a checkpoint, injuring a cop as he rode past.

Bourgoin-Jallieu, a large market town dear to my friend Florence, is rather sleepy this morning. On Main Street, where luxury shops stand shoulder to shoulder, I count only two or three young couples who, hand in hand, dream of designer garments on display in storefront windows flooded with light.

A woman in a wheelchair traveling on the opposite sidewalk notices us. Laughing, she salutes us, pumping her fist the way athletes do after a triumphant performance. We respond in kind. A sense of solidarity exists among the non-motorized.

Bénédicte, seized with a sudden urge, stops at a crossroads and wanders twenty yards or so off the road. While she's nonchalantly squatting down, a car suddenly screeches to a halt alongside me, which causes her to quickly stand back up. People often ask me whether long-distance walking is harder for a woman as compared to a man. Here's my answer for them: in terms of relieving oneself, yes, it is.

Narrow roads snake their way up hills so steep that we sometimes have to work together to hoist Ulysses up to the summit. It's at the top of one of these hills that we catch our first glimpse of the Alps' jagged skyline, bathed in bluish light. The village of La Tour-du-Pin is just as drowsy as Bourgoin-Jallieu, and no less so than La Bâtie-Montgascon, which boasts three cafes, a grocery, and a boulangerie. This sizable market town was once famous thanks to a very lively local politician, Gérard Nicoud,* a partisan of hardball tactics and

---

* TN: Gérard Nicoud (born 1947) ran a small bar-restaurant in La Bâtie-Montgascon. In the late 1960s and early 1970s, he was active in politics, defending the interests of small business-owners and artisans against big government.

an admirer of Pierre Poujade.* But today, no one knows La Bâtie-Montgascon anymore, nor its onetime hero.

The man running the bed and breakfast we check into for the night wanted to become a pilot. But having lost an eardrum in an accident, he was discharged from the Air Force. He became a pharmaceutical executive instead and bought himself two ultralights. Upon retirement, he earned his pilot's license for the helicopter that now sits out in his yard. It's a tiny craft for one person only. We're astonished by his passion for flying, and he's thrilled to hear about our odyssey. Happy are those who nurture dreams through many long years of work, then make them come true upon retirement.

As we close in on the Alps, we discover magnificent hilly landscapes crisscrossed by little flower-lined roads. It's a moment of bliss quickly quashed when a violent storm blows in. The roadway on which we're walking becomes a torrent, and our boots fill up with water. Bénédicte, who walks ahead of me and takes the celestial cloudburst with stoic resolve, shudders with each clap of thunder. In Novalaise, the only hotel is on holiday. We're going to have to camp through the succession of downpours. A woman out for a hike tells us that she would gladly let us stay in her garage, but that her daughter is celebrating her twentieth birthday in it with friends. We squat in a large shed on a farmerless farm. All night long, the showers and hail pitter-patter on the shed's metal roof.

The next day, as we're getting back on the road that rises to Col de l'Épine pass, a young blond woman with the face of a doll, fumbling with her cellphone in a pink bathrobe out in front of her house, answers our *Bonjour!* She then asks where we started out.

"In Lyon."

---

* TN: Pierre Poujade (1920–2003) was a populist politician. In the 1950s, he founded an anti-intellectual, pro-French Algeria, low-tax, and anti-immigrant movement, known as "Poujadism." Later populist movements around the world have been compared to Poujadism, such as Viktor Orbán's election in Hungary, the Yellow Vest movement in France, and Trumpism in the U.S.

"You've come from Lyon on foot? And where are you going?"

"To Venice."

"To Venice? On foot?"

"Yes," I tell her with a straight face. "We're on our honeymoon."

By the time she has pinched herself to make sure she's not dreaming, we're already long gone. Not quite a mile and a half down the road, a car passes us up, then screeches to a halt. From it springs the blond woman. She wants to take our picture and write an article. She asks us for our email address. Chuckling to ourselves, we go along with the idea. We never do see the photo, though. Perhaps, in the end, she didn't believe us. But we really are walking to Venice, though! And we really are on our first trip together as freshly PACSed lovers, spending all of our time with one another, which hasn't much been the case since we've been together, given how crazy our schedules are.

On the narrow, zigzagging road that ascends to the Col de l'Épine, a parade of vintage automobiles comes hurtling down the mountain in a roar. The sixty-something, graying drivers are clad in sporting attire: leather or motorcycle helmets, off-white driving gloves, and dark sunglasses. At full tilt, they take themselves for Formula One race car drivers. These "kings of the road" cut the curves . . . and come mighty close to cutting us off as they do. It's a foretaste of what we'll encounter later on, for all along the route we've chosen, as we pound the pavement, we have to fight cars for our share of the road. If we were to stick to the footpaths, our trip wouldn't take four months, but several years! For, outside France, they're rare. Long-distance hiking trails are a French invention that dates from the Revolution. After 1789, the government lacked the funds to maintain roads in thousands of French parishes. So it opted to maintain national roads only, while leaving secondary routes to the departments and footpaths to communes.* The communes pampered their trails. While

---

* TN: A French department (*département*) is a regional division (there are ninety-six in metropolitan France, and five overseas departments); a commune (*commune*) is the smallest French division (city, town, or village), and is headed by a mayor (*maire*).

in all other European countries, footpaths were abandoned or privatized—and, in some cases, annexed by farmers who thereby gained a significant strip of arable land—in France, hedges were pruned, brambles pulled out, and depressions filled in. And so today, with its thousands of miles of marked and passable pathways, our country is a walker's paradise.

Le Col de l'Épine rises to about one thousand meters (3,280 feet). The long descent ends in Chambéry, which, on this Sunday in August, is a ghost town. I phone Michel Grenier. A former teacher who loves hiking, he's a member of the "Chemins de Saint-Michel" Association, founded by Marie-Paul Labéy, an admirable woman whom I met a little while back on the old pilgrimage route from Rouen to Mont Saint-Michel.* Michel Grenier and his wife Michelle, both incredibly welcoming, offer us room and board for the night. Michel has also prepared a series of 1:25,000 maps to guide us all the way to Mont Cenis over footpaths. So we won't have to portage our gear, he selected trails that would be large enough to accommodate Ulysses's wheels. In the morning, Michel takes us back to the spot where he found us, that is to say, on a square nicknamed the "*Quatre sans cul*." Inspired by the "good ole days of the colonies," it's a colossal monument, representing four elephants' front portions, oriented to the four points of the compass. The absence of the animals' hindquarters explains why Chambéry's residents call it this.† Michel took friendship to a whole new level by marking on his map the best way for us to exit the city.

Autumn is already here: the morning air is crisp, the first poplar and wild cherry leaves have turned yellow, and some have dropped. Flowers appear to be making a last valiant stand. They've sprung up along the edge of the road in a final burst of color, in preparation for their long nap. At Étang de Carouge Campground, a

* See Bernard Ollivier, *Sur le chemin des Ducs*, Phébus, 2013.
† TN: The square is formally known as the Fontaine des Éléphants.

bittersweet, end-of vacation feeling hangs in the air. Last week, the supervisor tells us, the campground was 85 percent full; today, only a quarter of the sites are taken; and next week, it will shut down for the season.

Our arrival in the Bauges Mountains is a magical moment. Grapevines heavy with fruit scale the hillsides. In a few weeks, tractor-trailers will be running back and forth, carrying ripened grapes off to the cellars. A warm aroma rises from the soil and adds to the pleasure of walking. I try to ignore the sharp pain in my lower back, which has been bothering me from day one. I cling to the belief that, since walking heals all ailments, it, too, will soon pass. On the other side of the valley, near the main highway, some prostitutes are trying to lure motorists into a pitiful minivan for a quickie. These are the last signs we'll see of "civilization" before confronting the solitude of the summits towering overhead.

The road grows increasingly difficult. In certain, especially abrupt sections where we're unable to pull Ulysses up, we have to unload our backpacks and strap them on. With one of us pulling our load-lightened cart while the other pushes, we head up the steep grades. I admire Bénédicte who, in a contagious display of motivation and joy, never gives up when problems arise. Fond of good food, the edibles she pulls from her sack were prepared with all the skill of a nomadic chef. I'm moved by her stamina and good spirits. To think that I used to prefer solo journeys! The one I'm on now is making me more lovestruck with each passing day.

In the valley, we have to look way up over the treetops in order to glimpse the steep path that heads to our first real challenge: crossing the Alps by way of Mont Cenis.

II

FIRST BORDER

After the farm-covered Bauges Mountains, we reach the industrial Maurienne Valley and its aluminum smelters. The trail is sandwiched between the railroad, the national highway, and the mountain stream. Summer has just ended, the *gîte d'étape* is empty.[*] In the villages, children are no longer playing in the streets. They're in bookstores where they're spending the school year's best moments under their mothers' watchful eyes: buying school supplies. At Hurtières Lake, a young *Beur* just pulled from the water a carp weighing some eight pounds, which he then let's go.[†] All he's interested in is "catch and release": when he catches a prize fish, he weighs it, snaps its picture, then puts it back in the water. I ask him if he hopes to catch others. "I snagged the mother, so I'm looking for the grandmother," the easygoing fellow tells me, while adding that he doesn't eat fish.

Saint-Jean-de-Maurienne is a cyclist's paradise. Roads lead out from it like spokes of a bicycle wheel to ten or more mountain passes that figure on every champion's bucket list. Mont Cenis Pass, at 2,000 meters above sea level (6,500 feet), is said to be one of the easiest. While we're lunching out on a restaurant terrasse, vehicles go by that belong to the national cycling teams of the United States, Italy, and Ecuador. The city is decorated with white jerseys covered in red

---

* TN: *Gîte d'étape*: a self-catering shelter or refuge, typically in the mountains.
† TN: *Beur* is a colloquial French term for a European-born person with at least one parent (or grandparent) of Arab descent who immigrated from the Maghreb.

polka dots, just like the one given to the best climber in the Tour de France.

Mechanical trouble: a small steel cable that prevents Ulysses's wheels from doing the splits breaks. It's another *Beur* who offers me a piece of cable and lends me the tools I need. Two wonderful encounters on the same day, characterized by a sense of fraternity between travelers and homebodies. Does this augur well for what lies ahead?

In Orelle, there's not a soul in sight, except for two old women who think we're headed to Rome. Thrilled, they tell us how they had a brief conversation with a priest—either a Benedictine or an Oratorian, they don't recall—who's walking ahead of us to get to Siena. The campground is deserted. Since there is no host-camper, I drop a check into the letterbox at the Tourist Office. It's my first self-service camping experience.

In Modane, we stop briefly at a memorial commemorating those who died in the two European bloodbaths of the twentieth century. It bears witness for all time not to the glory of the combatants, but to the pain of "those left behind," the inconsolable ones. It portrays a woman whose upright posture expresses her great courage. An eternal tear, cast in bronze, wells up in a corner of her eye.

At the city limits, a section of GR5E, which travels through the Maurienne Valley,* bears the sweet name of *"chemin du petit bonheur,"* or "path of little delights." And the trail has indeed begun to work its magic. Walking among the flowers, the fir trees, and the beeches and oaks that are shedding their leaves at the approach of cold weather, a kind of peace of soul settles over us as we go along. In their little gardens, families are busily harvesting the last vegetables and pricking out winter salads. But the little delights of this first day of September are marred by a little problem: Ulysses's overused tow bar suddenly breaks. Yet it had been reinforced long ago

---

* TN: GR long-distance walking paths exist in several European countries. They are typically marked with a red and white cross. In France, the letters "GR" stand for *Grande Randonnée*.

in Uzbekistan thanks to a helpful welder and a piece of pipe recovered from a Russian tank. The Soviet steel held firm, but the tow bar broke right next to it. The only garage in the village that might help us weld our traveling companion's shaft back together is closed. Jonathan, who steps out from a cafe, fetches a drill from the trunk of his car along with a miraculous tungsten bit, and I manage to fix the problem temporarily. Jonathan works for an insurance company and is also quite the traveler. He attempts crude descriptions of those living in different French regions. "The people here are quite kind, just as they are in the Vendée or the Jura. But Basques," he says with a frown, "are like Corsicans."

At the Col du Mont Cenis, at an altitude of 2,083 meters (6,834 feet), our first border and our first selfie. Arms around one another, we act as if we've just conquered Mount Everest. The plateau is beautiful at this time of the year: blue thistle, bellflowers, and, we're told, eight varieties of gentians embellishing the shores of a large artificial lake whose water grows dark as evening falls. Bénédicte had suggested that we phone ahead and reserve a bed in the one and only gîte. "Nothing doing," I boastfully told her. "I'm a purist, out for real adventure." Now my partner ironically asks: "How much did we bet that all the beds would be taken?" For a group got there ahead of us, and there's no vacancy. Spending the night in a tent at over 2,000 meters doesn't exactly thrill the "real" adventurer who, only a short while ago, was blustering up a storm: it's chilly out. But by some miracle, the couple running the hotel *Les Roches blanches*, which was supposed to close this very night, agrees to work overtime at the request of the gîte's manager. The welcome is warm and the room cozy. I find all kinds of literature on the rich history of this border area.

In 1866, on the impetus of British engineer John Barraclough Fell, the English built the Mont Cenis Railway Company, which made it possible to travel from Lanslebourg in France to Susa in Italy in six hours, down from the twelve it took the stagecoach. This shortened time benefitted the *"Malle des Indes"* (The India Mail) service between London and Bombay, which passed through France. It was an enormous construction project for the time. The locomotive pulled six wagons: one first-class, two second-class, and two third-class. The sixth car carried freight. Since the line ran along precipices, the cars' small windows were located higher up to spare passengers suffering from vertigo. Just to be safe, seats were also turned inward, and travelers faced one another . . . just like in the London Underground.

This border plateau was also a place of confrontation between France and its transalpine neighbors. In 1888, following in the footsteps of an Italian initiative, an elite Army corps specially trained for mountain operations was deployed here, dubbed the "*chasseurs alpins*" (the Alpine Rangers). I also come across an old photo of a play the soldiers performed, terribly bored as they must have been in this remote location. The role of the friendly servant girl was played by a strapping lad with a mustache. Laughter guaranteed.

After the war, lines shifted. Since the Italians, allied with the Germans, had built a fort overlooking France, in 1945, it was tit for tat: the French, on the other side of the plateau, would now overlook Italian territory. Generals are always preparing for the previous war. A historian strolling about the premises tells us that General de Gaulle wanted to annex the Aosta Valley in 1945. There was a certain logic to his request, since a large part of the population in those days was French-speaking. But the Americans and the English opposed the idea. Mont Cenis became a major worksite yet again when, between 1962 and 1969, a dam bearing its name was built, along with a huge artificial lake and a high-powered hydroelectric plant. The supply of abundant, inexpensive electricity brought an influx of aluminum smelters, for they require large amounts of energy to operate.

On the morning of September 2, we travel along a section of the "Via Francigena," originally opened for pilgrims on their way to Rome. The trail is marked by the symbol tau (τ). It's the cross of St. Francis of Assisi. It lacks an upper section, and in some representations, resembles a coat stand topped with a dove. At intersections, the dove's beak indicates which way to go. The trail's descent into the Aosta Valley is steep and stony. We don our backpacks and Bénédicte, using a rope, holds Ulysses back whenever the slope makes it hard for me to slow down. More than ever before, we're working as a team, and I love it. We picnic out in the sun on a large boulder and gorge ourselves on wild strawberries for dessert.

In the narrow streets of the villages we pass through, little old ladies dressed in black revisit their youth by warming themselves in the sun. Bénédicte, more attentive to the details of people's clothing than I, points out to me that most women over fifty are wearing generous blouses or dark dresses, and that their canvas or leather shoes lack heels. The men, who sit apart from the women, use lots of gestures and speak in loud voices. Some converse in *Valdôtain* (Aostan French). The designation refers to a set of regional subdialects (or patois); in writing, it makes abundant use of the circumflex accent. One in five people in the valley still uses *Valdôtain* on a daily basis. Bruno, who speaks fluent French, explains that he chose to study our language in school since some of his family lives there. He traveled to southwestern France and was very impressed by the Montagne Noire region and that of Lézignan-Corbières, where he enjoyed not only the forest but also the wine. His rose-colored face suggests that this is probably true.

The Aosta Valley has always distinguished itself by a fierce desire for autonomy. Today, banners proclaim, "*NO TAV.*" The slogan is all over the place, on every facade and balcony. The entire valley is dead set against the *Treno Alta Velocità* (*TAV*), a high-speed train proposed between Lyon and Turin. It's a collaborative French-Italian project. It may be "high-speed," the project's adversaries point out, but above all, it's "high-cost": one hour gained for twenty billion euros—that's a lot of money per minute. It's a staggering project, with a tunnel over thirty-five miles long. The Valley, unified and unanimous in its opposition, is doing everything it can to delay the work: there are endless worksite occupations, demonstrations, and marches. It's easy to understand the opposition of these silence- and slowness-loving mountain folk. Young demonstrators in a tent city are busy painting slogans on large banners, getting ready no doubt for their next protest. A short distance away, a small wooden structure marks the exact location where the line will pass. Erected in 2005, it was burned by pro-*TAV* activists, but then immediately rebuilt. Luciano (ninety-two years old), Tomalino (seventy-six years old), Piera (seventy-seven years old), and Vicenzo (eighty years old) are holding their own. These four old-timers and their friends take turns occupying the site day and night, all year long. In the cabin, a wood-burning stove, installed for the coming winter, serves to heat up coffee and food. Newspaper clippings attest to their combat; letters bear witness to the fact that they've maintained regular contact with the "*Zadistes*" opposed to the construction of the Grand Ouest Airport in Notre-Dame-des-Landes in Brittany.* The talented Italian writer Erri De Luca,† who called for the worksite's "sabotage," wound up being sued by the company. But he didn't care and, when a journalist asked him: "Are sabotage and vandalism lawful?" he replied: "They're necessary to underscore that the *TAV* is a toxic and useless project." The rebellious writer, faced with a possible eight-month prison sentence, told the judge that were he convicted, he wouldn't appeal the verdict and would serve his full sentence. On October 19, 2015, he was acquitted.

In Susa, the Franciscans of the Casa Francisco advertise that they welcome both "pilgrims and non-pilgrims." And indeed, the place is as comfortable for us heathens as for a woman kneeling before a wooden statue of Christ. No one says a "benediction" before the evening

---

* TN: The construction of the Grand Ouest Airport at the Notre-Dame-des-Landes site near Nantes, originally proposed as far back as 1963, received the green light from the government in 2008. Environmentalists and others strongly opposed to the project occupied the site, which they referred to as the "*ZAD*" (the *zone à défendre* or "zone to defend"). Anti-airport activists squatting the site became known as *Zadistes*. In 2017, the Macron government reconsidered the project, weighing yet again its pros and cons, and, in December 2017, decided to definitively abandon the project.

† Born May 20, 1950 in Naples, Erri De Luca is a notable novelist, translator, poet, and political activist.

meal: Bénédicte, who loves to eat, is delighted by just how tasty and profuse the dishes are. The rancid butter at breakfast, though, means our hosts will lose the five-star rating we would otherwise have given them. On the road, we get into the habit of picnicking before our siesta; we vanish into some sunken lane and savor sandwiches composed of a winning trio: *mozzarella di bufala–mortadella–pomodori.*

In each village or hamlet, it's customary to post death notices on display boards, usually accompanied by a photo of the deceased. Old-timers consult this death gazette while out walking their dogs. People do not die very young in the Aosta Valley: most of the departed are at least seventy-five years old, with the exception of a lovely young woman named Sylvia, who was only seventeen.

III

OUR ITALIAN CAMPAIGN

Perched atop a peak, the Sacra di San Michele is often compared to the Mont-Saint-Michel on account of its impressive size, but also because the Abbey is under the protection of the same devil-defeating archangel. Abandoned for a time, it saw the monks return in the nineteenth century. It's rumored that Umberto Eco drew inspiration from the site in writing *The Name of the Rose* (*Il nome della rosa*). The large building—it takes an hour and a half to reach it—is so imposing, appearing either ominous from the outside or secure from the inside, that three days after having passed it, its proud profile is still visible on the horizon.

The traffic is growing increasingly heavy. How can we continue on this course? If France is a walker's paradise, Italy, home of the immortal Fausto Coppi, is that of cyclists.* Here, two of each year's most celebrated events are the Tour de France and the Giro. We're tempted to travel on bicycle paths since there are no GR routes in Italy, but that's impossible since they've generally been designed as one-way loops so that pedalers never have to see the same asphalt twice. We have no choice but to stick to the *Strade Statali*, Italy's state highways.

---

* TN: Fausto Coppi (1919–1960), the "Champion of Champions," was one of the world's greatest cyclists in the 1940s and '50s. He won the Giro five times and the Tour de France twice.

For the first time, Bénédicte feels afraid. I'm not as averse to heavily traveled roads. I took them quite a bit when I walked the Silk Road. I'm living proof that a pedestrian on a busy highway has a reasonable life expectancy. If that weren't so, I'd have been dead for the past fifteen years! Still, I must admit that the traffic between Tehran and Xi'an isn't the same as here. Especially since Italians drive like mad and one in three motorists has a cellphone glued to their ear. I introduce Bénédicte to survival rule number one: always walk on the left, against traffic, so that you can see the truck and the truck can see you. As the miles go by, countless little shrines by the roadside bear witness to those who met their deaths violently in car-related accidents. The victims are mostly young. The mechanical monster craves tender flesh.

So off we go into the stream of cars, Bénédicte out ahead, me behind, pulling Ulysses. We purposefully turn north so as to avoid Turin, a big industrial and commercial city, which, to pedestrians like us, represents a rather significant obstacle. In a village, we hit it off with a joyful group of young people who, seated comfortably at a table outside a restaurant, are reinventing the world. They're impressed by our undertaking. We ask them if they know a place where we can sleep. We're tired, and the nearest hotel is two miles down the road. A young man gets up and says he'll ask whether their parish priest might put us up. He comes back looking sheepish. The holy man asked:

"Are they going to Rome?"
"No, to Venice."
"Then no, I don't want them."

When you set foot in Italy, you also step into history. On our maps are familiar names: Lodi, Castiglione, Arcole, Rivoli, Bassano, Verona, and more. I can't get enough of walking where others have trodden in search of glory, riches, or their little corner of heaven. Visions of pilgrims hoping to win paradise and those of long caravans winding their way through Asia's deserts carried me all the way to Compostela, then on to Xi'an. Here, we're following in the footsteps of Napoleon's Great Army, whose superiority, historians tell us, was due in large part to the speed and enthusiasm with which his foot soldiers marched out onto to battlefields and to their death. The French may have thought that they were liberating the Italians from Austro-Hungarian occupation, but they were not welcome everywhere. In the Veronese Easter rebellion, the local population rose up against the French in a bloodbath. To avenge his soldiers, Bonaparte drove out the Doge of Venice, whom he held responsible. French soldiers set fire to the immense boat from which the republic's "monarch" tossed a gold ring each year into the deep, in celebration of how the city was wedded to the sea. The soldiers even tried to recover all the gold with which the vessel was profusely decorated.

At an intersection, a little drama. A car is stopped. Seated next to it is an old man in a wheelchair, with scratches all over his face. He's watching an old woman—his wife—rummage through a large brier. She tells us that, in an attempt to satisfy a sudden urge, her husband lost his balance and fell headfirst into the brambles. His glasses fell off in the accident, and she's unable to find them. Sharp-eyed Bénédicte spots them. We get back underway, as they shout *Grazie mille!* over and over.

We're gradually settling into the itinerant lifestyle. The stress of the first few days—fear of a reluctant body and about walking as a couple—is gone. *Tutto va bene.* It took us longer to cross the Alps than planned, so I'm quite certain now that we won't make it to Venice on schedule. But why do we have to go all the way to Venice? We'll pick up next year wherever we left off. Isn't the journey more important than the destination?

And the journey is pleasant. We lunch on simple, tasty dishes, seated outside, in the shade of trattoria pergolas. As she licks her fingers, Bénédicte repeats over and over that these little roadside restaurants could teach those back in France a little something, so many of which now practice the art of freezer-to-microwave cuisine. After a half-bottle of light-bodied wine, our heavy legs carry us to a patch of grass or a shady public bench where we take a restorative nap. We still haven't been able to pick up more detailed maps, one of the main reasons being that the notion of the "region" is by no means hollow here: maps of Lombardy aren't sold in the Piedmont, and vice versa.

For a taste of a little silence—at the risk of getting lost—we head into the rice paddies. Bénédicte has never seen an ear of rice. Since I admired a good many of them when in Asia—in a minuscule attempt at settling scores with my partner, who knows far more about botany than I do—I revel in showing off my knowledge of these large, canal-bordered squares brimming with stagnant yellow water and swarming with mosquitoes eaten by countless frogs which, in turn, fall prey to hundreds of herons and egrets. There's not a soul in sight. It feels a bit like the Wild West.

Vast farms—or *casale*—are like entire villages unto themselves. Each has a church or chapel. The manor house is the only building that's more or less maintained; all the others look ready to collapse. They call to mind the extraordinary film *Riso Amaro*, with the lovely and provocative Silvana Mangano, a testament to those not-so-distant days when landowners brought hundreds of women in from the South to transplant rice seedlings.* The film's raw realism; the outfits of the women, in water up to their thighs; the violence exuded by the characters: it was all quite thrilling to French filmgoers of the 1950s, who were then just discovering Italian cinema. The days of pricking rice seedlings in by hand are past, tiles have blown from the massive dormitory roofs, and the landowners stop by only briefly these days for the mechanical harvest.

We're quickly lost. Here and there, we come across a loafing dog. But we come up short in our search for a human being who can get us out of this labyrinth of canals and stony pathways, which Ulysses's

---

* TN: A film directed by Giuseppe De Santis and released in 1949. English title: *Bitter Rice*.

tires loathe. I'm busy grumbling about Bénédicte and her bucolic yearnings when our savior suddenly appears in a cloud of dust: it's a parish priest in a white Fiat *Cinquecento*. Hosanna! He sets our sights on a church bell tower, we exit the rice paddies, and now we're in the city of Novara.

It's no tourist town. On this Monday morning, all the storefront shutters are down. The countless surveillance cameras film but a handful of passersby. Bénédicte has received a message regarding a theatrical performance at the start of the school year and needs to find a computer. Internet cafes have entirely disappeared from our cities, rendered useless by the ubiquitous smartphone. We're sent from one street to the next until someone finally directs us to City Hall where, we're told, we'll find what we're looking for. And indeed, a charming young woman shows us in and places a phone call. Her face lights up with a smile, and with a thumbs-up, she lets us know we're in luck. Our delight, however, is short-lived, for she then explains the following protocol:

a. Submit a written request in an office down the hall for permission to use a computer in the technical center. To do that, we have to go to the waiting room and bide our time.
b. Once we have the document, we have to head to the tech center on the other side of the city to be sure that the operation we'd like to do is possible.
c. If the tech center determines that our request is acceptable, we then have to come back to City Hall for the green light from an employee who will take payment in advance for the equipment rental.
d. Receipt in hand, we then have to return to the tech center to check our email.

In the end, not far from the train station, we stumble upon a French-speaking Moroccan who operates a small internet cafe with a dozen computers. The fellow is clearly discouraged by his enterprise's limited success. Later on, we walk past an office that we recognize to be the tech center: a long queue of tourists is impatiently waiting for two overwhelmed employees to attend to them. Kafkaesque!

IV

THE NAVIGLIO GRANDE

In Novara, we embark on a quest for a more suitable roadmap. To no avail. A young and likeable bookstore employee suggests we follow the Naviglio Grande Canal, whose construction began in the twelfth century. It served two purposes: to carry water to Milan, but above all, to transport the enormous blocks of marble needed for the construction of the city's breathtaking cathedral, the way the port of Saint-Dyé was built on the Loire River to carry stones to the Château de Chambord. Our rescuer points out that the canal will guide us directly to the cathedral square. What more could we hope for? Overjoyed at the idea of walking for two days without a single car to bother us, we head for the road—rather congested, unfortunately—to Ponte Nuovo, where we can access the Naviglio. The bridge there is yet another to have played a crucial role in the Napoleon saga. In 1859, Napoleon III crossed the Alps, seeking to confront the Austro-Hungarian Army at Magenta. He hoped to use the three bridges straddling the Naviglio Grande. His enemies, caught on the defensive, were short on time and only managed to destroy two of them. The Franco-Sardinian Army crossed over the Ponte Nuovo, the only span still standing, and headed to victory.

From atop this famous bridge, we lovingly contemplate the canal. A towpath runs along the left bank. We lower Ulysses down onto it to offer ourselves a picnic beside the water. Far from all the noise, we give in to a nap before getting back underway, following the current. A few cyclists pedal nonchalantly by; joggers return our greetings of "*buongiorno!*" with a smile. People stop to ask where we're from, where we're going, and—a sign of the times—for our email address. The pathway has a small, paved section on which Ulysses can roll freely along, and a grassy section that's soft beneath our feet. To the right and to the left stand lavish residences. Most of them are empty, testimonies to past splendors.

As the evening wears on, a countryman suggests that we spend the night at a nearby farmhouse that practices *agriturismo*. It's a form of countryside accommodations that we'll opt for on several occasions. We take a wrong turn, and it costs our tired legs dearly, but it's all quickly forgotten when, after twenty-eight miles on the road, we finally reach Laetitia's guesthouse farm. Her barns house five hundred cows and calves. She graduated from the Sorbonne with a bachelor's degree in French five years ago, and then became . . . a yoga instructor. The rental apartment is decorated with simplicity and good taste. Laetitia Monti is a sensitive, talkative woman who takes a few moments before dinner to say grace. We question her at length about Italy's political situation and about her life. She tells us of the difficult times she has been through recently, losing five of those nearest and dearest to her in two years: "The house was full, now the house is empty." She prepares an excellent meal: zucchini, braised pumpkin, *Viande des Grisons*,* and of course pasta, "cooked a little more for the French than for the Italians." She has two daughters, one of whom opens her home up to troubled teens. Laetitia has traveled far and wide: to South America, and to India, where she goes every year. She's just back from a discovery tour of Tuscany, whose beauty left her in awe.

It's Erika, Laetitia's second daughter, who serves us breakfast before we head back to the canal. Vehicle traffic on the right bank is so heavy that we progress more quickly than the cars. It's a joy to be able to thumb our noses at them! Beautiful houses give way to

---

* *Bündnerfleisch*. Seasoned, air-dried beef. A Swiss specialty, named for the Canton of the Grisons where it is produced.

community gardens. Here, just like back home, the economic crisis has triggered renewed interest in gardening. A mason tells us that he has been out of work for many months and asks us what his chances might be of finding a job in France. Laetitia told us that her children, who put in long years of study, are worried they won't find jobs. Berlusconi, whose unpredictable zigzagging is messing with democracy, isn't, in her view, doing much to help.* As for the financial situation, some claim that Italy is experiencing a crisis similar to that in Greece. It's the summer of 2013 and the country is depressed.

We're almost to Milan when Ulysses breaks a leg. A bolt that holds his left wheel on has broken loose. After a few difficult miles, the owner of a bicycle shop rummages for a long time through a catch-all box, eventually coming up with a replacement bolt we can use. He refuses to take the least centime. Ulysses's homemade appearance, I suspect, enchants all those who work with their hands.

The canal's starting to look like it's on vacation. Along its banks, trattorias cater to a noisy clientele. The Italian language is as suited for speaking as it is for singing. As promised, the Naviglio Grande leads us straight to the square in front of Milan Cathedral, the Duomo, dedicated to Saint Mary of the Nativity. An architectural marvel as only engineering backed by faith can sometimes produce. It's the third largest church in the world! The structure, begun in the fourteenth century, has given rise to so many enhancements that the work has never stopped. From the outside, the visitor is struck by the building's amazing height, which reaches to well over three hundred feet at its peak, but even more so by the incredible number of statues that stand on its roofs, and which transform the building into a gothic hedgehog. It's impossible to visit the Duomo without climbing to the top in order to zigzag your way through its many

---

* TN: Silvio Berlusconi (1936–2023), Italian Prime Minister from 1994–1995, 2001–2006, and 2008–2011. Member of the Chamber of Deputies from 1994–2013, then member of the Senate. Leader of the Forza Italia party from 2013–2023, he was convicted of tax fraud in 2013.

works of art. The cathedral has over three thousand of them, two-thirds of which pierce the skies. The highest is the Madonnina, a golden statue that overlooks all the others. The tradition was that no building in Milan should ever be built any higher. Two powerful companies defied the law in a crafty maneuver that enemies might have once called "Jesuitical": they installed copies of the Madonnina on their roofs. I'm moved most of all by the tiny statue of a dove whose marble has suffered a bit from the elements. The patina of time adds a touch of poetry to the bird.

V

SOLFERINO:
THE BLOODY HILL

Hardly interested in trudging through an insane amount of traffic, we exit Milan on a little commuter train, then hop off in the first village whose name escapes me, although I cannot forget that of the excellent dish we order in a nearby restaurant: *Pranzo di Lavoro* (The Workers' Menu). It consists of three delicious dishes served on white linens beneath an ivy-covered arbor. My word, these Italian *lavoratori* are given the royal treatment! We then take a siesta on a couple public benches in a small park on the way out of town.

Today's road is a bloodthirsty highway, buzzed as we are by the worst drivers of all, those busy making phone calls. Unfortunately for us, a large horse show means there isn't a single vacant hotel room for fifty miles around. We camp off the highway under a large oak tree. Throughout the night, a pack of dogs keeps us awake and we notice a little light pattering on the canvas. Is it rain? That would be surprising, for the sky was clear at nightfall. In the morning, mystery solved. The tree above us is infested with thousands of caterpillars, and the clumsy ones fall from the leaves they're munching on. They're all over the tent, and on the ground.

In the village of San Paolo, Alberto, whose vermillion face reveals his appreciation of Italian wine, bluntly calls out to us: (To Bénédicte) "Where are you from? Where're you going? On foot?" (To me) "And you, how old are you? Seventy-five? I'm seventy-one. We're a couple of tough fellas, wouldn't you say?" (To Bénédicte) "And how about

you? I won't ask your age, that's not polite, but do you have kids?"
Then, having gotten all the news, which he'll no doubt broadcast
throughout the village, he takes leave of us, satisfied. A little farther
along, a young jokester in his car slams on the brakes in front of us
and pokes his head out the window: "Are you taking on passengers?"
We're still laughing even after he drives off.

Our overnight at Frederika's house is both costly and disappointing. But we can't expect to run across a Laetitia every day! Our young
hostess has been bitten by the consumerism bug and is hooked on
modernity. Her apartment is a showroom of uncomfortable furniture
and ostentatious decor. She's covered from neck to ankles in tattoos
and tells us that her life's dream is to buy a literary cafe. Sadly, she's
neither moneyed nor cultured. She blushes and looks down at the
floor when she tells us that she works in a dental prosthetics lab.

We advance in zigzag fashion, eager above all to avoid life-threatening roads. From time to time, we find a little bliss beneath our
boots, such as from Manerbio to Leno. For a five-mile stretch,
a tiny and enchanting road winds its way through cornfields and
prairies, then sinks beneath a canopy of foliage that shades us from
the oppressive sun. We navigate between two rivers. The one on our
left accompanies us all the way to Leno, while the one to our right,
which is really just a canal, flows in the opposite direction. Chirping
birds, grasshoppers, insects. Tree frogs that plop into the water at our
approach: we stock up on this inhabited silence, for we'll soon be
back on a busy road—Bénédicte's bane—although little by little she
gets used to it.

The road offers us Grazia and Romeo. He's tall, standing a good
eight inches over her. She's as radiant as the sun. Wanting to know
how to get to Castiglione, we strike up a conversation. Grazia urges
us to visit the church over there on the hilltop—it's *bellissima*—as
well as her home village, which she loves so much that she never goes
on vacation unless she absolutely has to. We chat for nearly two miles,
then Grazia invites us into her nearby house for coffee. She won't let
us leave until we have her phone number, just in case. Romeo insists

on guiding us to the edge of the village. The afternoon is just as pleasant. Cyclists greet us and motorists wave their arms in a show of solidarity. In the countryside, many *cascine* are in ruins.

As we approach Castiglione, I think about the countess of the same name who, it has been claimed, was the nineteenth century's most beautiful woman. Victor-Emmanuel, future king of Italy, sent her to Paris to facilitate the rapprochement between his country and France. A scandalous, seductive spy, she was a sensation. Men quivered at the thought of her satin sheets. She enticed Napoleon III into her bed. Did the affair have a decisive influence on the agreement reached between the two nations that led to Italy's independence and France's acquisition of the Savoy and the city of Nice? The Countess of Castiglione added a few more princes to her list of conquests; then, worried about growing old, had herself photographed hundreds of times in breathtaking dresses only to finally withdraw from the public eye, ashamed of the ravages of time.

This market town has but one hotel and we're its only guests. The next city conjures up another event that was to have a lasting impact on human history: The Battle of Solferino. The site is well worth a detour of a few miles. But it comes at the cost of a steep climb, which means hauling Ulysses up to the top, too.

No less bloody than those before it or those yet to come, it's a battle that would hardly be worth our time except for the fact that, for once, it had a positive outcome. The Austrians had fortified the highest hill overlooking the village: consequently, it's only on account of the French Army's superior artillery that Napoleon III's soldiers were able to emerge victorious. It was a bloodbath. After the withdrawal of the armies' troops, estimates put the number of the dead and wounded at around thirty thousand. Henry Dunant, a Swiss citizen who had arrived on the scene, was horrified. Men were groaning and dying in the field. There were only six French military doctors. Stretcher-bearer corps were nonexistent. So he set up a makeshift hospital in one of Castiglione's churches, although it could accommodate no more than five hundred of the wounded. He succeeded in convincing military leaders to let captured Austrian doctors attend to the maimed as well. He later told how moved he was by the dedication of Italian women who spontaneously came to the victims' aid, regardless of the side on which they had fought. In response to his stupefaction, the women replied *"tutti fratelli"*: all brothers! Unable to forget what he had seen, three years later, he published at his own expense *A Memory of Solferino*. He ordered just over a thousand copies, then sent them throughout Europe to people who shared his aversion to war.* One year later, on February 17, 1863, he and Frenchman Frédéric Passy founded in Geneva the International Committee of the Red Cross. In honor of Dunant, its flag is an inversion of the Swiss flag: a white cross on a red background. He believed that a wounded soldier could no longer be considered an enemy and must therefore be protected and treated. He would later extend such protection to prisoners of war. Perhaps because he had carelessly devoted all of his time and money to the cause, Dunant made some bad business deals and was convicted of bankruptcy fraud. He was forced from the International Committee of the Red Cross and took refuge in Heiden, a tiny Swiss village, until his death in 1910. He was the recipient of the first Nobel Peace Prize, in 1901.

At the top of the hill, built around a central monument, is a wall engraved with the flags of signatory states to the Geneva Conventions for the Red Cross and Red Crescent. Down below, on the small village square, the facades—many of which stand atop beautiful arcades— are of that ocher color that so nicely blends with roof tiles and the Italian sun. At tables outside a restaurant, diners speak in loud voices and make copious use of emphatic gestures. After so much brooding over bloodshed and cannon fire, we find these peaceful sounds incredibly melodious.

The landscape has changed. Corn—omnipresent for several days now, indispensable for animal feed—has disappeared. There is an

---

* TN: J.-Henry Dunant. *Un souvenir de Solférino*. Geneva: Imprimerie Jules Guillaume Fick, 1862.

abundance of fruit: apples, peaches, kiwis, grapes, olives, pomegranates. The Radamez *Agriturismo* is beautiful and peaceful. The owner, Alfonso, a tall, smiling young man, has laid out the family farm with exquisite taste. While showing us the small studio where we will sleep, our host mentions that the bottle of white wine in the refrigerator is a welcome gift. It's one of those places where, during breakfast, you think about how hard it's going to be to leave. Alfonso wears three hats: he's an architect, a B&B manager, and a wine-grower. The grape harvest begins in a few days; it's an event that will require a great deal of his attention. Later on, when we're ready to leave, he insists that we take a bottle of red wine from his own vintage with us. It's a real struggle to convince him that, in a backpack, a bottle of wine would go bad and, above all, would be very heavy.

Is it the white wine—which, incidentally, is excellent—or the fatigue? Something takes place that evening that I had long been dreading and which I won't soon forget. Alfonso suggests that we dine in a restaurant out in the middle of nowhere and lends us two bikes to get us there. So off we go on the narrow, winding roads of this very hilly region. I'm tired and lag behind; Bénédicte rushes on ahead. We begin an endless downhill section, and I start worrying that it's going to be a tough climb back up. We're clearly lost and Bénédicte, who doesn't like depending on others, refuses to stop for directions. We start to argue. We can't find the restaurant, so we head back to the gîte, still hungry. I'm furious. I can't understand why my mate would stubbornly keep pedaling when she has no clue where she's going. Some of my most interesting encounters have taken place when I stopped to ask for directions.

We heat up a can of green beans then go to bed angry, refusing to talk to one another. It's our first argument since we've been a couple. The storm broke after thirty days on the road. I'm awake most of the night. Travel puts you through the wringer, it lays your soul bare. You can put on a good face in public, but when you have to cope with so much exertion, discomfort, and a constant lack of privacy, cracks and fissures appear. Fatigue forces you to take off your mask.

Is this that infamous curse of journeys begun together but finished apart? Are we, too, going to split up, breaking the powerful bonds that bind us?

The next morning, when we sit down for breakfast, we enter into a frank discussion, which we carry on for the first few miles of the day's leg. It's vital that we understand what it was, on both sides, that ended in incomprehension, anger, and a quarrel. Love very quickly restores harmony. Prior to this, I often boasted to Bénédicte: "We've known one another for six years and still haven't argued: what's up with that? All normal people argue from time to time! Why don't we?" Since that fateful evening, though, I crow a little less and keep from repeating that now meaningless refrain.

Bénédicte, who's passionate about gardening, is eager to reach Valeggio sul Mincio. Within the limits of this small city is the vast Parco Giardino Sigurtà—Sigurtà Garden Park. Its developers have modestly labeled it *"il più straordinario giardino d'Italia"*—Italy's most extraordinary garden. Its one hundred and fifty acres are a true work of art and are, once again, a testimony to the Italians' incredible eye for Beauty. The site's layout; the way the plants, wetlands, and trees are organized; the colors and fragrances: everything has been done in a show of exquisite taste. Bénédicte is in seventh heaven. A stage actress, in the warm season, she performs in a show that takes place in gardens. In vegetable gardens, that is. It's called *Paradisi Hortus*, inspired by the works of great writers. Our visit here is such an intensely pleasurable experience for her that we find ourselves regretting the tight schedule we're on, which forces us to return to France by a certain date. A short stay in a neighboring *agriturismo* farmhouse would have put her on cloud nine. The Sigurtà also holds a place in history since Napoleon III stayed there, having chosen it for his headquarters during the Italian campaign. Surrounded by so much beauty, could a man even imagine the dreadful bloodbath he had set into motion only a few miles away?

A scenic lookout bears the name of Juliette, as if to remind us that we're nearing Verona, the homeland of those who harbor such great love, they're ready to die for it.

After photographing this sublime location from every imaginable angle for our future desktop backgrounds, we go from silence into asphalt hell. There are no verdant roads heading into Verona. I'm tense; I keep a close eye on the cars rushing headlong toward us. If I yell, Bénédicte mustn't try to see or understand why, she needs to simply jump into the ditch.

While we're having a rest at an intersection, a fellow named Pascale comes over to us, pushing his bicycle alongside him. He works all day long on a computer and spending time out in his garden helps him relax. He's on his way back from it now with a large plastic bag on his handlebar: from it, he pulls two succulent peaches and offers them to us. Probably thinking that his gift isn't enough, he takes out a smaller bag full of ripe figs and insists that we take the entire thing. It would be wonderful to get to know him better, but already our timetable is breathing down our necks. Maybe next year?

As if right on cue, Ulysses's left tire bursts smack dab in front of the signpost proclaiming "Verona," our final stopping place this year. I'm very tired. Replacing an inner tube while cars zoom by not far off makes me nervous. So we push on to the hotel rolling on the rim. The tire winds up in shreds. After two agonizing hours, accompanied by the nasty sound of metal on pavement, we stop at the first hotel we come to. It happens to have four stars. Ulysses crosses the lobby like a king, pulled by a porter in full uniform and white gloves.

We don't have much time to see the sights, but there are two gems in Verona that mustn't be missed. The Roman Arena, unfortunately, is being readied for a concert and its doors are closed. In a tiny courtyard, a tightly packed, impenetrable crowd snaps photos of a balcony, that of the immortal Juliette. On the stairway leading up to it, excited young women wait their turn to make an appearance while their Romeo prepares to take a souvenir photo from below. We flee the throng.

Luigi Licci is a tall man with the build of a condottiere. He's the owner of the Gulliver–Libri Per Viaggiare Bookstore. Crazy about travel literature, he gave up his former career as an insurance agent, though it paid better, for this bookstore. Luigi, who speaks flawless French, asks if next year, before we get back underway, I would join him for a meet-and-greet with readers of the Italian translations of my books. I gladly accept.

Lino Francescon works in Brussels for the European Union. He vacations each year in his hometown of Padua. He was so taken by my Silk Road travelogue, his bookseller in Brussels told me, that he gifted the first volume to fifty people or so, leaving it to them to buy the other two volumes. He puts us up and has us visit Padua, a city whose every street corner he knows like the back of his hand. In the Scrovegni Chapel, we have to elbow our way through the crowd to admire Giotto's exceptional frescoes. Sublime shades of blue, daring compositions: we're overwhelmed! It's one of the most beautiful works of the Italian Pre-Renaissance period.

The Palazzo della Ragione (Palace of Reason) stands at the heart of the city. Built in the thirteenth century, it's an imposing building. The ground floor is, in fact, a covered market where we once again admire how skillfully Italian merchants showcase their goods. How marvelous these southern markets are with all their fresh vegetables, whereas those sold in most supermarkets and hypermarkets back home are already withered by the time they go on sale. A walk through these alleyways does wonders for the appetite.

But what's truly marvelous is one floor up. An immense room eighty-one meters long by twenty-seven meters wide, beneath a ceiling twenty-seven meters high (266 ft × 89 ft × 89 ft). Which makes it the largest room that's not at ground level anywhere in Europe. Six or seven tennis courts could fit inside. On the walls, paintings represent the seasons and the signs of the zodiac. Initially painted by Giotto, they were destroyed in a fire, but replicas, identical to the originals, have since been created.

In a corner of the building stands a large, round, black stone whose top is shaped like a stool; it's the *Pietra del Vituperio*, the "stone of shame." Insolvent debtors were sentenced to sit atop it in shirt and underwear, and in the presence of one hundred people, to repeat the formula *"cedo bonis"* (I give up my possessions) three times before being expelled from the city and formally forbidden from ever returning, unless their debtors consented. The sentence was introduced at Saint Anthony of Padua's request: it replaced the terrible physical abuse previously inflicted on those who failed to pay their debts.

Italians are very skilled at preserving their immense cultural heritage. Everything in Padua is beautiful, without ostentation. To stroll about its arcade-lined streets is to wander through history. I meet the owner of Pangea, a bookshop which, like that of Luigi Licci, specializes in travel literature. Having learned of the event organized by our friend Lino, he too would like me to meet my readers next year, and we set a date.

We go for a cup of coffee at the famous Caffè Pedrocchi. Prepared in the secrecy of the kitchens, it's a hot-and-cold blend of subtle sensations: coffee, chocolate, and crème de menthe. It's truly divine. Embedded in the *caffè*'s wall is a chunk of lead. Care was taken not to disturb it, even when the walls were repainted. The Caffè Pedrocchi, a center of resistance against Austrian occupiers, was popular with student protesters. The stray projectile was fired by soldiers during a particularly turbulent demonstration, which ended in a number of arrests.[*] Out on the square, the marinated octopus vendor has finally arrived, so we head over to enjoy a platter, washed down with a glass of Tokay.[†]

---

[*] TN: The Habsburg rule in the Kingdom of Lombardy-Venetia in the early- and mid-nineteenth century. The student revolts referred to here took place in 1848.

[†] TN: Better known today as Friulano. A white wine made from a grape known as *Sauvignonasse* or *Sauvignon Vert*, among other names. It is produced in Italy's Friuli region.

And so, in the light of a magnificent sunset, our stay in Padua comes to an end.

See you next year, *Bellissima!*

PART TWO:
VERONA TO ISTANBUL

THROUGH
BÉNÉDICTE'S EYES

In discussions with friends in the weeks preceding our departure, the only topic of interest was the "adventure" we were preparing. Consequently, many of them asked us to keep them informed of our progress online. That's something I don't do. Though my family and friends are frequently on my mind when I walk, I remain focused on the journey at hand, and care little for writing postcards. I'll gladly share the tale, but only *after* I'm back home.

During this second year, Bénédicte—twice incapacitated and forced to stop walking—took up writing newsletters to her friends. Timidly at first, then decisively. By the end of the journey, it was a delight to see how focused she was on one of her chronicles, which had grown more frequent and jubilant. After having recapped several days on the road, my "*poucette*"* would pick up the cellphone and patiently send little text-message "postcards" describing what she had seen and felt, all written in a voice that, if not always refined, was lively and natural. Our friends, eager to find out what happened next, kept asking for more. Only after our return home did I finally look these chronicles over, since I can't stand reading on a cellphone. I then managed to convince my partner to slip them here and there into the narrative I had written, since I was supposed to be our journey's official diarist. I regret today that she only took up writing

---

* TN: *Poucette*: one of Ollivier's terms of endearment for his partner, along the lines of "Thumbelina." In the plural, *poucettes* are "thumbcuffs": indeed, Flatet's use of the cellphone keeps her thumbs busy.

during the second half of our adventure: I'm certain that her eye was better than mine for the thousand things that escaped me between Lyon and Verona.

* * *

Setting Out—July 29, 2014

Back from the Avignon Festival,* I quickly buckle up my pack. I pull the door closed for the next four months and, with each turn of the key, wonder what I'll wish I'd brought with me, and what will just be extra weight. Why did I ever suggest to Bernard, two years ago, that we hike this final leg of the Great Silk Road? We could simply have stayed home and kept ourselves busy watching our tomatoes turn red, comfortably stretched out on our lounge chairs. . . .

Yet we are encouraged by the 560 miles we traveled last year. The crash test of walking side by side for one full month didn't do us in, and I received my diploma in long-distance walking from the hands of Bernard Ollivier himself! But the Balkans are an entirely different kettle of fish. And 1,250 miles is no stroll in the park.

With thoughts racing through my mind and ready for anything, I leave tomorrow with the love of my life, my heart brimming with our friends' warm affection. I've promised to send them news.

And I have butterflies in my stomach.

So be it. This is where the adventure begins.

BF

---

* TN: The *Festival d'Avignon* is an annual summer arts festival that takes place in and around the city of Avignon, located on the Rhône River in southern France. Many of the performances and workshops revolve around theatre, Flatet's specialty.

VI

EXHAUSTION

July 29, 2014. Departure is always a tearing away from something. In a few minutes, we'll board the train for Paris, then a second for Verona. Bénédicte is engrossed in her computer. One minute more, Mr. Killer of Time, despot of the moment at hand. Out my side, in front of our meadow, I catch one last glimpse of the trees I planted five years ago. This spring, they shot new, fragile leaders skyward. In four months, having lignified, they'll be ready to continue their upward climb with the return of warm weather. I ponder yet again what compels me to leave when my life at home in Normandy is so harmonious. You have to make up your mind. To close the door. Farewell little nest house! In the silence of the fall, it will await our return.

In the train today, July 31, there's a rush of vacationers. Two-thirds of them—I hope—will have wonderful encounters and forge new connections; but right now, they're deaf and dumb, with their eyes and ears in their MP3s, computers, and cellphones.

In Verona, Alessandra, a kind young journalist sent by our bookseller-friend Luigi Licci helps us settle into the Corte Carolina farm guesthouse and interviews me for a local newspaper, *L'Arena*, which, the following day, publishes a full-page story titled: "The Philosopher of the Road."* Waiting for departure is

---

* Alessandra Milanese. July 31, 2014. "Io, da pensionato finito a camminatore filosofo," *L'Arena*, Verona, Italy.

a trial for me. Mentally prepared for what awaits us, my legs are raring to go. We have to bide our time until tomorrow morning's departure. We stroll through the city, which we enjoyed exploring for the first time last year. And we quickly settle into our ritual: *caffè* for her, cappuccino for me. Beneath the arcades on the other side of the Via Adigetto, a woman performs—with closed eyes—a beautiful rendition of a Bach sonata for violin. It's her livelihood. In the land of the arts, the artist's life is no bed of roses. A short distance away, a legless woman is propelling a customized bike. Right behind her is a little girl on a tiny bicycle; then papa, pedaling along and towing a baby carrier: in it, their wide-eyed newborn is discovering the wide world. Nothing is impossible for those who want to go places.

This evening, Luigi has set up a meet-and-greet for me with my Italian readers in the little town of Zevio, near Belfiore, where the "Goose Festival," a musical and literary event, is currently underway. It's a well-known city, for Maria Callas's first husband was born here, and a museum dedicated to the diva's life is under consideration.* The reception I'm given by the 150 or so people is warm. Luigi does a fine job translating for me, since my Italian hasn't improved a bit since last year. A lot of people want to meet the madcap who walked 7,500 miles from Istanbul to Xi'an in China. But once again, I notice that what my admirers are most surprised about isn't the athletic feat itself, but the fact that I set out alone. Even Gianni Sirotto, the get-together's moderator and daredevil adventurer who took every imaginable risk in the mountain ranges of Europe and South America, always set out with a friend. Put my life on the line? Sure. So long as there's someone with me.

After a short, rainy night, we say goodbye to Gemma and Paolo, our charming hosts at the Corte Carolina. This is it, then. Destination: Istanbul, 1,250 miles down the road. Providence willing, that is!

---

* TN: Maria Callas (1923–1977), American-born Greek soprano.

Ulysses is back up and running after getting a major tune-up from my friend Marcel Lemaître. The habits picked up last year reassert themselves in no time. It's the hiker's routine: securing our packs on our cart, then the first steps on the road until we come to a bistro. Espresso for her, cappuccino for me. Each time, the waitress sets the espresso down in front of me, while Bénédicte gets the cappuccino, with a little heart drawn in the foam. As if cappuccinos were meant for women: but I stand by my choice! We head down a little road nearly hidden between two canals and thronged with people: cyclists decked out as if for the Tour de France, joggers, or walkers. We suddenly hear: "Bernard! Bénédicte!" A woman and her friends who were at the reception in Zevio last night form a circle around us and ply us with questions. But we have to get going!

On the way out of Verona, in a suburb called Lepia, stands a large commercial building that was supposed to revolutionize the region's shopping experience. One hundred yards long, sixty wide, and four stories, surmounted by citadel- or penitentiary-like square towers. Upon completion, two years ago, a publicity and media campaign billed it as the event of the century. Six months after opening, the verdict was in: the almighty customer had not been lured by parking lots as large as football fields, complete with specially built access roads. The building has already fallen prey to time: it's a brand-new ruin. We stop for a moment to contemplate this rather ironic commercial catastrophe, the pitiful result of consumerist madness.

Next to it stands an old monastery. It, too, has been abandoned: bamboo and ivy have invaded its walls. Bougainvillea bushes soften the place's sad look, but the conventual buildings have nearly all collapsed. All that remains is a campanile, but the bell used to summon the faithful to mass has been removed. Everything here is falling apart, both money and religion!

Late in the day, we cross over the Torrente Alpone, a tributary of the Adige, which is spanned by the famous Arcole Bridge.

Given that it's being repaired, we won't be able to set foot on the prestigious stone bridge where Bonaparte made his mark. A temporary steel footbridge has been erected for local pedestrians until the work is complete. On the riverbank, an obelisk of sorts commemorates the famous event. It's struck with Napoleon's letter "N" and is surmounted by the Imperial Eagle. No doubt because the Italians are more familiar with the emperor than the Corsican general, the inscription reads: *"Monumento a Napoleone."* Admittedly, eight years prior to being coronated emperor, *"Buonaparte"* was already revealing the *"Napoléon"* in him. In classic French naïveté, in history class, I imagined that, spurred by the fervor they felt for their hero, his soldiers launched an attack and immediately captured the whole area. What really happened was somewhat different. Though our Corsican hero did indeed rush forward onto the bridge, in a hail of gunfire, he managed only to get halfway across. His Grenadier Guards whisked him off to safety a short distance away. Those protecting him—his aide-de-camp and General Robert—paid with their lives. The span was finally taken, but only through a ruse worth recounting here. Bonaparte ordered his drum corps to wade across the river and skirt around the Austro-Hungarians' rear flank, then sound the charge as if they were heading up a relief column. The enemy general fell for it: he sent some of his troops back to protect his rear, which he believed was under attack, weakening his defenses. Despite his twenty-five thousand men as compared to the French forces' nineteen thousand, the bridge was taken, and the enemy defeated. In war, only the outcome matters.

Though at Solferino, as we saw, the battleground and Red Cross monument draw quite a few tourists, Arcole is a less-frequented site, such that it even lacks a hotel in the downtown area. Despite a grueling day, we have to walk several more hours to find a guesthouse; at first, the owner tells us it's closed, but seeing our sullen faces, he agrees to let us have a room for the night. To get to a restaurant, we have to travel a never-ending mile each way and then some, despite

being worn out. We've covered nearly twenty-two miles in all, sheer
madness for a first day back on the road.

We have a hard time getting going again in the morning, for our
muscles have yet to eliminate all of yesterday's toxins. But little by
little, the endorphins kick in and we make it to noon without a hitch.
Like last year, encounters are few. People are wary at the sight of
two strangers with an odd-looking vehicle. We're approached by an
old man only: he asks us our nationality. From her porch, an elderly
woman, conversing in a stentorian voice with the man next door at
his window, shouts "*Turisti!*" to him upon seeing us, then fails to
answer our greeting. After a hearty meal in a trattoria, a nap is in
order. Near Orgiano's War Memorial, we drift off to sleep, using our
hats as pillows. On the memorial, whose boundaries are marked by
four large shells pointing skyward and linked together with chains, I
count sixty dead in the wars of 14–18 and 39–45, and an additional
twenty killed in the Russian campaign alongside the Germans.

Setting out again, we embark on an inevitable state highway, a
strada statale. Trucks brush past us dangerously. But a small road,
which ought to lead us to Abetone, promises shelter from the noise
and mechanical fury. A farm with a wide-open front gate looks like
an inviting place to fill up on water. An old woman napping on an
armchair, two forearm crutches within reach, dismissively points us
to a pipe they use to water their livestock. The front door suddenly
flies open, and Roberta rushes out into the yard. All smiles, she asks
us what we wanted, and sets about preparing glasses of ice-cold water
flavored with mint, into which she drops a few large lemon slices.
She beams with happiness at this apparently rare encounter on her
isolated farm. She has such good teeth that they could appear in a
toothpaste commercial. She was busily reducing her garden tomatoes
into sauce for the winter. She drops everything and strikes up a conversation with the same energy she puts into her work: she wants to
know where we're from, where we're headed, and she tells us about
her much-adored only child, who will soon be back from London

after completing a language program, and who has hiked the Way of St. James. "She is beautiful on the inside," the woman concludes. She asks us to take a souvenir photo before we head off again. Out in the yard, the grandmother—who has finally understood that we're walking—asks: "Did you take a pilgrim's vow?" Roberta, meanwhile, turns to Bénédicte and asks: "Do you have a son?"

A short while later, we go past a courtyard, the walls of which are cluttered with a thousand different statues and haut-relief figurines. Two men are conversing beneath an arbor, and they motion us to enter. The sculptor working here has a fitting surname—Giacometti*—and a little less appropriate first name—Armando. Self-taught, the faces he sculpts in white local stone exhibit striking naiveté; they reveal uncommon creativity and a keen eye for character. In the wall between his house and the road, other faces emerge, imprisoned in the stone like victims of a curse.

The evening wears on without the slightest chance we'll find a gîte or hotel to sleep in. Surrounded by irrigation ditches, the plots of land are all hard to access. After a long search, we set up our tent behind a house left half-done: the economic crisis hasn't affected shopping malls and monasteries only. We'll see many more unfinished structures like this farther along. In a spot somewhat secluded from the road, which isn't heavily traveled anyway, we sleep better, but not enough to fully erase yesterday's fatigue. I'm angry at myself for having made a rookie's mistake, as it's hard on my wife. The air turns hot and humid, and it wakes me up. A storm's a-brewing. At 6:30, we decide not to wait for it to reach us and pack our bags. As we head out, the first drops start to fall, then the sky empties itself out in a roar.

Luigi sent us a message informing us that Giacomo, a reader of mine who was at the reception in Zevio, would like to walk this stage

---

* TN: Like Swiss sculptor and painter Alberto Giacometti (1901–1966). After studying in Geneva, Giacometti moved Paris in 1922, where he lived and worked much of his life. His artwork is heavily influenced by cubism and surrealism.

along with us, and the fellow has also offered to put us up in Padua.
We arranged to meet in the city of Albettone, which is along our route.
Unfortunately, we get lost, tricked by a parallel cycling path that sucks
us in for quite a while before we finally realize that we've gone astray.
We wander about in the rain for nearly two hours. At an intersection,
we try stopping cars for directions, but it's no use: we observe yet again
how cautious Italians are in dealing with foreigners like us. In the end,
it's a woman who, looking down at us from her truck, tells us which
way to go. We find Giacomo sipping coffee in a service station. He's a
tall young man of twenty-nine, sporting a trendy three-day-old beard;
he has a very gentle look in his eyes, which nicely complements his
slow diction. He's recently back from a big trip: he hitchhiked from
Verona to Hong Kong, then returned home on the Trans-Siberian, a
five-month tour. We get back underway, grateful that we have him to
guide us, for the route to Padua wavers between countryside and city
along small, unmarked roads. Every house bears the sign *"ATTENTI
AL CANE"* (BEWARE OF THE DOG), which speaks volumes about
local hospitality. We're so tired that when Giacomo suggests we go for
a *pausa gelato* a few streets from his house, we both have great difficulty
getting up from our couch and using our legs again: they're heavy
and stiff as cement. We finally reach Giacomo's house at seven o'clock,
and after over twelve hours on the road, we're completely spent. Sheer
madness for a third day. I start thinking how I was a little too opti-
mistic about the distances we'd cover. Thankfully, our hosts revive us
through their kindness, thoughtful gestures, and comfortable bed.
Ilaria, Giacomo's love interest, is a slender brunette employed in the Far
East fabrics trade. They attended the same junior high in Italy without ever bumping into each other, then finally met in Beijing. They
both speak perfect English. Ilaria, in addition to knowing Chinese,
expresses herself in French with ease. After a long-overdue restorative
night, we're joined by our two new friends for our second visit of the
marvelous city of Padua.

    We meet up with our friend Lino Francescon, who was on a trip
in Tuscany but decided to come back early rather than miss us. With

him, we head over to see Giandomenico in his bookstore, Pangea, for the meet-and-greet he organized for my Italian readers. Eighty attendees squeeze into an underground room intended for forty! They all fan themselves for a little oxygen. It's a convivial gathering; the attendees, who give us a warm welcome, are exhilarated by the touch of exoticism we bring.

It's the morning of August 7, and regretfully, we have to bid Ilaria and Giacomo farewell. We should have extended our stay with this marvelous couple so as to make the most of our newfound fondness for one another, and to catch our breath. But it's not easy for me to quell the Capricorn within. He's the one I blame for my tendency to push on ahead, even when it means missing out on some of the journey's pleasures. And as far as my drive to travel far and fast is concerned, Bénédicte, alas, is more of a gas pedal than a brake. Our two friends accompany us this morning to the canal we'll follow all the way to Venice. Giacomo insists on pulling Ulysses. The two ladies walk out ahead: Ilaria, erect on her feet and relaxed, advances with soft steps alongside Bénédicte, who's more alert and deliberate. Walking styles fascinate me, as they're often indications of character. I'd love to make a documentary that would initially show people walking from behind only, before revealing their actual personalities. I'm no physiognomist, but from behind I can recognize a man from China, the Netherlands, or from North or South America; an English woman, who tends to walk pigeon-toed; a Parisian woman, who waddles like a duck; a deceitful man; or an inhibited and shy person.

When we reach the canal, it's time for us to part ways. Ilaria, whose eyes twinkle with intelligence and affection, holds back a tear. We're all overcome with emotion: though brief, this has been an incredibly rich and warm encounter. For these young people, whose life together has only just begun, our intrusion has brought a whiff of the adventure they crave, though the need to secure their professional futures stands in the way.

VII

VENICE AND TRIESTE

Beneath a buttermilk sky, we set course for Venice, and first of all
Mira. For a few miles, we follow the *Cammino dei Giusti del Mondo*
(The Way of the World's Righteous). Small stone slabs honor those
who came to the aid of civilian war victims in Armenia, Rwanda,
and the Balkans, including Bosnia. As we go by, I notice the name of
Anna Politkovskaya, a journalist killed because she refused to keep
silent.

Both sides of the Naviglio del Brenta Canal are lined with
patrician villas, each attempting to outdo the others in terms of size,
rich decor, and elegance. Built for Venice's wealthy merchants—and
in proportion to their owners' egos—they were proof of success.
Boats would arrive and tie up at the foot of the houses' large marble
staircases, which climb to colonnaded entrances. Each has a sumptuous ground floor characterized by high ceilings, then a second floor,
reserved for the owners. The uppermost floors accommodated a size-
able household staff. Today, most of these large houses display only
the faded finery of former glories. But one, the Malcontenta, has
been designated a UNESCO World Heritage site. As I make my
way toward the *Serenissima*, I cannot help but dream of the glory
of that city, which—if I'm to believe my idol Fernand Braudel—
dominated world commerce for eight centuries and brought to the
Mediterranean region a number of business techniques, including, at
the end of the fifteenth century, the revolutionary practice of dou-
ble-entry bookkeeping. The city gave the world an example of an

oligarchic form of government that answered not to a god, but to the Doge's peers.

To reach Venice, we have to go by sea. Although there's room for Ulysses in the small boat that carries us from the little port town of Fusina to the city by the lagoon, not so in the *vaporetti* that serve the Grand Canal, for our cart would take up three seats all by itself. That's unthinkable in mid-August when tourists fiercely lay claim to every last square inch of these large water taxis. We're turned away. And so, since foot travelers we are, we will travel the city on foot! We wear ourselves out just trying to get up and over the Ponte dell'Accademia. We resort to our Alpine technique: we don our backpacks and, with one of us pulling our cart while the other lifts or pushes it, we make our way as best we can to the Cannaregio neighborhood,* where our friend Annie is waiting for us. A few years ago, Annie sent me a very nice letter after having read one of my books. In closing, she offered to put me up, were I ever to come to Venice. I took her at her word.

We hurry along, dodging a thousand obstacles: alleyways so narrow it's hard to squeeze past someone coming the other way, and small bridges and side streets along secondary canals in which noisy, compact groups of tourists leave no room for anyone else. We finally get to Cannaregio where our friends unearthed for us a small, perfectly equipped apartment near the Campo Santi Apostoli. A charming terrace, enclosed by a picket fence, offers direct access to the canal, just like nearly all Venetian homes. The Cannaregio neighborhood where we're staying was formerly the Jewish quarter. In fact, the term "ghetto" originated here in Venice. It's most likely a deformation of the word "giotto" or "geto," which meant "foundry," since that was the industry in this district.

Annie, a mosaic artist, was born in France. At the peak of the season, she and her Italian husband Enrico flee the tsunami of tourists—the city of sixty thousand hosts twenty-five million visitors

---

* TN: Venice's northernmost historic district.

each year—and hole up on Sant'Erasmo Island, whose core business is supplying the city with fruits and vegetables. They stay in a one-time lighthouse now converted into a rental home. As a welcome present, Annie has brought us figs from her summer island, and we immediately gobble them down.

After an eagerly awaited shower, we head off in search of a trattoria that Ilaria recommended. The entree, made from a pumpkin base, is simply divine; and don't even get me started on the *panna cotta*—the taste is still vivid on my tongue.

On August 9, as the heat dies down and the tourists, exhausted after miles of wandering the city streets, are making their way back to restaurants and hotels, Annie and Enrico knock at our terrace gate. They suggest we take their little boat for a Venice water tour. Enrico—Rico to his friends—was born here and knows the city through and through. As we exit the tiny canals, he points out the houses where Wagner and Carlo Goldoni resided, and a woman by the name of Desdemona, from whom Shakespeare drew inspiration. Not until the sixteenth century, Rico tells us, did city merchants have their palaces built of stone. Previously, the buildings' wood and cob facades were painted. Some still bear the traces of ancient frescoes. While skillfully steering our boat through the tiny canals or amid the Grand Canal's heavy traffic, Enrico lays out for us the city's eight golden centuries until its final collapse, caused in large part by Bonaparte in 1797.

I find in Venice few vestiges of its former silk industry, once so prosperous, just as it had been in Lucca, Genoa, and Florence after Sicily's near-monopoly.

It was in fact a Norman, Roger I, a contemporary of William the Conqueror, who was responsible for capturing the Kingdom of Sicily and encouraging the development of silk-making techniques there. Christians and Muslims, who lived in harmony on the island, mastered the art of raising cocoons and weaving silk; they turned Sicily into a hub where the rest of Europe flocked to buy the noble fabric.

Though unsuccessful, Roger I endeavored to secure a monopoly over its trade. There wasn't a lot of competition between the Italians and the French, given that the former specialized in heavy cloth for making furniture, whereas Lyon's focus was on producing lighter fabrics for garment-making.

At the end of this exhilarating two-hour visit, we moor the boat to one of the many large pilings sunk to the bottom of the canals. Annie, with a knowing smile, opens a trunk and pulls out four glasses and a bottle of Erasmus, a sparkling wine produced on her island. We clink glasses. It's a precious moment. In the soft twilight, we feel embraced both by the beauty of this place and by the warmth of friendship. As night falls, our hosts head home to their island, after first dropping us off in front of our terrace door. Tomorrow, the real fun begins as we set out for Trieste and the border.

We had to take a boat to get to Venice, and so we leave the city in the same way. It takes us an hour of sailing to reach Treporti, at which point we get back to our walk. It's a radical change. Venice was full of foreign tourists, but here, it's the Italian working class, on endless, identical beaches. Bénédicte and I treat ourselves to a first: a dip in the Adriatic. But it isn't easy for us to reach it! The Italian beach concept overemphasizes the instinct of private property. Each group brings along all the amenities: food, tables and chairs, inflatable mattresses, loungers, radios, mothers-in-law in armchairs, beach games, dogs, beach umbrellas, pillows, and more. The place is correspondingly loud: radios blare, then shouts and lively conversations take over; the latter are in turn drowned out by loudspeakers, over which messages or advertisements are broadcast.

We move away from the beach hoping to find a campground somewhere quiet, but here, silence is unnatural here. Between the motorhomes parked alongside one another, voices, screams, and television sets send a storm of piercing sounds into the hot, muggy air.

Setting off again, we actively search for a parallel path some distance away from the beach, for that would free us from having to travel overcrowded sidewalks. We come across one that wends its way between vacant fields. Down below we spot a few houses and a most-welcome metal workshop. For several days now, I've been concerned about Ulysses's tow bar, which, back in Modane, already snapped once. It's a thin steel pipe subject to considerable stress at the point where it's welded to our vehicle's undercarriage. Over time, the tube has become bent. Just one hard jolt and this fragile spot would give way completely. In the workshop, Oswaldo is busily categorizing pipes. Burly, with horn-rimmed glasses, a helmet of white hair, and mostly hidden behind a large leather apron that's seen its fair share of fire, grease, and grinding-machine sparks—as a true professional, the man understands my gestured explanations perfectly; still, he hesitates. His boss isn't there and the shop's supposed to be closed for summer holidays. He finally gets down to work. He straightens the tow bar with two blows of an enormous hammer, cuts two strips of metal which he welds on, and *voilà*: Ulysses is once again ready to handle the strains of the road. Oswaldo won't let me pay him, he won't even take a tip; stretching out his calloused and leathered hand—the result of a long apprenticeship with steel—he intimates that a hearty handshake is worth more than a few euros.

The traffic is so heavy out on the road that, after two or three close calls, we decide to get lost so we don't lose our lives. With a finger to the wind as our compass, we turn down a small asphalt road. Very quickly, it turns to dirt, then tall grass, and we struggle to pull Ulysses, whose wheels and belly become bogged down in the vege-tation. Just as we're starting to doubt that we'll wind up anywhere but the middle of a field, we pass a couple out walking their two dogs. They reassure us: we are indeed on the road to Caorle. They ask questions, show their surprise, and gape in amazement. "What a pity you're going *that* way, 'cause we live *back there*," the woman says, pointing in the direction from which we've come. "We'd have loved for you to stay at our place." Aside from Ilaria and Giacomo, it's the first time anyone offers to put us up. They act surprised. "You know, people are only wary because you're not familiar faces." We head off again, filled with optimism and confidence in human generosity.

Bénédicte comes to a sudden standstill: she feels a stabbing pain in her left knee. An hour later, despite a little rest in the shade of a large tree, the pain returns, worse than before. We have to take another break. We seize the opportunity to dry out our tent which, soaked from overnight condensation, was stewing in its juice. When the pain doesn't let up, we decide to stop in Caorle, halfway to our destination. Tomorrow, we'll have only a little over nine miles to go, and that way we won't overtax her painful joint. We'll fall a day behind our walking schedule, but to hell with saving time. What's most important is that we avoid jeopardizing the rest of the journey. We left Lyon with the firm intention of reaching Istanbul: we're not about to stop in Caorle. One good night in a hotel, a swim in the Adriatic, and, if needed, one full day of rest will have her feeling better.

But if it's rest you're seeking, Caorle, a popular seaside resort, is hardly the right destination. Around the hotel, which sits directly on the sea, crowds spill forth as thick as if someone had called a demonstration. The clamor of these thousands of vacationers—shouting to one another, yelling, laughing, and singing—is constant. Out our room window, on the third floor of the building across the way, dozens of slot machines rattle away, children scream, and all the windows are wide open. It's a plunge into working-class humanity, a triumph for the mass consumption of goods and recreation. And it lasts until four in the morning when the drunkards raise a stink about the bars closing, and the police finally put an end to it all.

In the morning, we get back on the road and set a slow pace. Bénédicte's worried the pain's going to return. It starts up again after six miles. Frequent breaks, stretching, plenty of water—the best remedies for tendonitis—but is it tendonitis? We confer. We had planned to spend the night in Lugugnana, but we'll push on a little farther to Latisana, where there's a train station. Bénédicte will travel by train to Trieste and wait for me there while taking care of her knee. I'll do the three stages between here and Trieste alone. My companion's morale is in the dumps. She has long dreamed of us traveling together, and now, just six days in, her body is already refusing to cooperate. I reassure her. I've been there. During the first few days of a walk, a sharp pain always crops up in my left thigh, as if a nerve were suddenly too short. But the endorphins eventually kick in, the pain subsides, and I can keep going.

It's a short night and, on the morning of our separation, Bénédicte goes with me to an intersection where we regretfully say our good-byes. I set off down a long, straight road, and each time I turn around, there she is: tense, trying hard to smile. In that moment, we become keenly aware of our love for one another. It's only a three-day separation, but her gentle spirit is deeply wounded. The blasted straight line goes on forever. Each minute, I glance over my shoulder and her ever-shrinking silhouette waves as if to hold me back. It occurs to me that I'm being a real jerk, and that, despite her refusal, I should have insisted on spending these three days with her and taken her to the doctor. But this walk is a joint affair: by continuing on foot, I am, in a sense, walking on her behalf. And then there's that blasted Capricorn in me, telling me to push on and on and on. . . .

The road seems endless, but based on the distance markers, I notice this morning that I'm traveling at almost four miles per hour—not too shabby for an old man. The thought that I'm seventy-six often gets me doubting my own abilities. City after city, country after country, I have to keep convincing myself that I really do have what it takes to make it to the end.

Walking solo is an entirely different game. As a pair, people seemed indifferent to us; but now, intrigued by my appearance and by Ulysses, they call out to me: they want to know where I'm from, where I'm going, and, once the ice is broken, how old I am. I tossed two T-shirts into my pack before leaving. The one I'm wearing is a souvenir from 1996, when I ran the New York Marathon. It displays the colors of the French flag. That's not always a good thing. A cyclist riding past, one who no doubt bears a grudge against my country, flips me off with the back of his forearm in that infamous

Italian salute which the French call *le bras d'honneur*. I salute him more modestly with a *doigt d'honneur*: my finger. Could he be one of those idiotic nationalists, of which there are so many now popping up across Europe, who fail to understand that this is the kind of hatred, dictated by shortsighted political ideology, that led us into the last world war? I experienced that one firsthand and have no desire to experience another. And it would be all the more unforgivable in that Italians living around Trieste witnessed the rise of nationalism in the neighboring Balkans and saw for themselves the human devastation it wrought. This cyclist's behavior is atypical, though, and most interactions I have are warm and friendly.

In a trattoria for lunch, I'm enjoying a tasty platter of pasta—the kind of slow energy a walker needs—when several people come over asking questions. They stepped out of the bar next door, where I had first gone in search of a meal. The bar's owner, a fluent French speaker, doesn't serve food, so he sent me to the trattoria, but only after subjecting me to a probing interview. His curious customers now want to confirm what he reported back to them. A skeptical woman asks my age. When I tell her, she doesn't believe me and gets very angry, thinking I take her for a fool. Amused, I show her my passport. She stretches out her hand: "*Braaavo!*" While others, raising their eyes to the sky, exclaim: "*Porca miseria! Madonna! Auguri! Complimenti!*"*

I was starting to think I could make Trieste in one day. I lack a reliable map, so I rely on road signs to gauge distances. Well, this morning, leaving Cervignano del Friuli, a signpost indicated that Trieste was forty-one kilometers (25.5 miles) away. After a week of warming up, it's a distance I'm no doubt capable of, so I get to thinking that I'll be able to meet up with Bénédicte this evening. All I have to do is skip the stopover in Sistiana: I should be able to travel the distance in seven or, at the most, eight hours, taking extended breaks. So here I am on the road at only 6:30 in the morning. I set a quick

---

* TN: Bravo! Holy shit! Mother Mary! Best Wishes! Congratulations!

pace and am merrily sailing along toward Bénédicte. I've been on the road for over four hours and have covered at least twenty kilometers (12.4 miles) when, as I'm making my way down an endless boulevard through the town of Montfalcone, I stumble upon a sign that reads: *"TRIESTE, TRENTACINQUE CHILOMETRI"* (35 kilometers or 22 miles). Drats. The sign back in Cervignano was wrong. And now the weather starts acting up. A heavy storm blows in, followed by a second downpour. My morale goes to pot. Depressed, my legs like lead, I finally reach Sistiana. I won't see my love until tomorrow after all. She phones. The pain's abating, the city's beautiful, and she's picked up a few maps for the rest of our journey.

While I'm eating lunch, a couple at the neighboring table strikes up a pleasant conversation. The man, whose first name is Alberto, offers to take me on a tour of Trieste tomorrow morning. Of course, I won't be there yet since, from the looks of it, I still have twenty-five kilometers (15.5 miles) to go. Too bad, he tells me, since by afternoon, he'll be on some beach in Croatia. He walked a ninety-mile portion of the Way of Saint James and plans to one day continue all the way to Santiago. When we part company, he tells me with a smile that his last name is easy to remember: Borgia.*

In the morning, I avoid taking the coastal route, which carries especially heavy traffic, and head for an inland road that will lengthen my journey slightly, but worse, will force me to climb to the top of the hill overlooking Trieste. Thick, black rain clouds burst open, one after another. I usually hold up pretty well in downpours, but when the road becomes a footbath, I throw in the towel and go for shelter beneath an arcade. A motorcyclist on the other side of the street did the same thing. I can't make up my mind which of three roads to take, as none are marked. A man, who just purchased his

---

* TN: As in the House of Borgia, a noble family that originated in Spain. In fifteenth- and sixteenth-century Italy, the Borgias became influential in political and religious spheres, producing, for example, two popes. The family was, however, no stranger to scandal.

daily paper, smiles and, having guessed my destination, points to one of them. I ask for confirmation:

"Trieste?"

He nods in agreement. I hesitate, for the street he's pointing to is the narrowest and seemingly the least traveled. My disbelief must be written all over my face:

"Do you speak English?" the man asks, who then, speaking that language quite well, assures me that it is indeed the road to Trieste.

Chilled to the bone from the storm I just got caught in, I drop into a nearby bar. The man follows me and introduces himself: Filipas, a retired sailor. He has had stopovers in Marseille and Le Havre and insists on paying for my cappuccino.

To get to Trieste, I'll have to race back down the thousand feet I've been climbing for the past two hours this morning. The slope is so steep and the path so wet that, at times, Ulysses drags me into skids that I have a hard time controlling. At one spot, the roadway, hemmed in by two ditches, has turned into a lake nearly sixteen inches deep, and when I reach the other side, I have to empty out my boots. I meet up with the coastal road. Bénédicte and I are supposed to rendezvous at the train station around noon. As I'm advancing along the sidewalks in order to avoid traffic, I hear someone yell "Bernard!" From the road, a motorist is waving at me. It's Alberto Borgia. He was so intrigued by our journey that he decided to skip his day of Croatian *dolce far niente* and has been driving up and down the coastal highway hoping to spot me. He insists on taking us on a tour of his city. We arrange when and where we'll meet. At the train station, I give Bénédicte a big hug. This three-day separation has been tough on us; not once did she leave my thoughts. Is the pain in her knee going to ease off, or will we have to cut our journey short? For the moment, my partner is fine.

Alberto—quite the chatterbox with his mix of French and English—gives us a tour of the recently opened War Museum for Peace. Its creator assembled thousands of objects: rifles and pistols, clothing, posters, photos, and the enormous cannon that occupies part of the courtyard. Each display denounces the absurdity of war, the massive sums of money it requires, the misery it generates, and the hardships endured on both sides of the front.

That evening, we dine in Sgonico, a village high above the city, surrounded by hills riddled with karstic caves—limestone formations known for their many deep cavities. During the last war, scores of war victims were thrown into them, transforming them into great, makeshift mass graves. Tomorrow, it's a day of rest for me and a supplemental day off for Bénédicte. We eat lunch with Matteo and Cristina. They've heard about the Seuil Association from mutual friends of ours, Luigi Nacci and Alberto Conte, who organize a literary festival in Monteriggioni, Tuscany, to which I was invited last spring. Matteo and Cristina recently tied the knot, an obligatory step before they can adopt a baby. Since the organization's objectives are dear to them both, instead of gifts, they raised funds to benefit Seuil. Salaried employees of an NGO that guides asylum-seekers in applying for refugee status, they help immigrants from Iraq, Syria, and Afghanistan find housing. That's no easy task in a country that, among European nations, has been nearly alone in having to cope with the flood of refugees, some arriving by land, as here in Trieste, others by sea in Lampedusa.

We say our goodbyes to Alberto, Cristina, and Matteo, who've helped us get over the lukewarm welcome we received in Italy after crossing the Alps. This evening, we're keenly aware that the Po Valley has in fact been the easy part of our journey. Beyond Trieste lies the unknown, and walking will become much more difficult: tomorrow, we'll finally set foot in the Balkans, a word that, in Turkish, means "mountains."

* * *

Trieste, August 14

Trieste. Springboard to the Balkans. Just 124 miles from Verona, but for me, a little less, since I had to give a reluctant knee some rest. And two speaking engagements for Bernard in Verona and Padua, where he was a big hit.

The day after tomorrow, we leave Heavenly Italy and its magnificent chaos, sumptuous cities, and flamboyant culture; its language as delectable as its ham, cheeses, vino, pasta, *and* caffè *(ah! its* caffè, *unlike any other!). And, of course, its ruins, unfinished houses, and crowds of commoners packed so tightly on the Adriatic's beaches that you lose sight of the sea; its omnipresent* Lega Nord,* *its electric gates, barred windows, and guard dogs that bark at us; its doors, which remain closed. Except that of Roberta and her unforgettable smile, who offered us glasses of grenadine on a torrid summer's afternoon; and that of Giacomo and Ilaria, whom we met at Bernard's first conference, and who put us up in Padua.*

We're in the land of the well-to-do, just like in France, where opening one's door to strangers—however much like cousins they are, the way we ought to be for the Italians—is by no means a natural reflex.

But what would I do—what would YOU *do, reader—if two not-so-young wayfarers were to knock on your door and ask point-blank if they could spend the night? I honestly don't have a clue. In which case . . .*

What kind of welcome will the Croatians and Bosnians give us with our sunburned faces, our less-than-presentable threads, and our gypsy cart, on which we hang our socks and underwear out to dry?

You'll find out in the next episode!

BF

---

* TN: The *Lega Nord*, or *Lega Nord per l'Indipendenza della Padania* (or simply, LN) is a right-wing/far-right political party in Italy, known since 2018 simply as the *Lega* (the League).

VIII

THE MOUNTAINS

August 17: a dramatic change of scenery. We set foot into a swarm of nations, most still licking the wounds of a civil war marked by religious and ethnic hatred. A region where, not long ago, people risked death not for what they had done but for who they were and what they believed. A region where, beneath the skulls, bloodthirstiness still smolders. And finally, a region that, while attracted to Europe, drags its feet before accepting its rules.

This hard-to-reach region has been shaped by a complicated and violent history: it's a land of passions. From early on, each local potentate imposed his personal religion. Some of the population—the Slavs—came from the North, while others came from Turkey. The Ottoman Empire occupied the region for several centuries. The Slavs imposed Christianity, the Turks Islam, and Eastern Christians orthodoxy. Conversions took place depending on the outcome of battles, at sword-point. The explosive mix of origins, religions, and cultures resulted in constant fighting, and it was all the more horrific in that it forced people living in the same country, village, or neighborhood—sometimes even in the same family—to do battle with one another. Throughout history, people have torn one another apart here, either in the name of a particular land, or in that of a god. Simplifying a bit, the Balkans enjoyed two periods of relative calm under the iron rule of authoritarian regimes: occupation by the Ottoman Empire and, closer to our own experience, unification under Tito. Religious ideas are the region's main source of trouble, but not the only one. Hunger for power and nationalism have played key roles as well.

In 1912 and 1913, the so-called Balkan Wars broke out, due both to a weakening of the Ottoman Empire and the Christians' desire to be free. In June 1914, Archduke Franz Ferdinand, heir to the Austro-Hungarian Empire, was assassinated along with his wife by a pro-Serbian anarchist, Gavrilo Princip: it was the spark that would plunge all of Europe into war. In 1918, the Kingdom of Yugoslavia was formed, reuniting Serbians, Croatians, and Slovenes. But peace was fragile and, in 1939, all the Balkans entered the war. Leading the fight against the Axis Powers, consisting of the Italians, the Japanese, and the Germans, was a Croatian communist activist, Josip Broz, more commonly known by his assumed name: Tito. When the region was liberated, he waved his iron fist, swept away disparities, and created a new state from the ground up: Yugoslavia. He stood up as much to the West as to Moscow. He was one of the founders of the Non-Aligned Movement, that is to say, the refusal to side with either of the superpowers, the United States or the USSR. It was, moreover, in Brioni—Tito's hometown—that, in 1956, a meeting took place with Nehru of India and Nasser of Egypt that would lay the political foundations for the Non-Aligned Movement, a kind of syndicate designed to let emerging nations speak their piece without becoming too involved or ensnared in East-West confrontation.

Tito's death in 1980 was to have dramatic consequences. In 1991, after ten years of rising temperatures, the Yugoslavian pressure-cooker finally exploded. Slovenia and Croatia proclaimed their independence; Macedonia followed suit. In 1992, the Bosnian War broke out. Ethnic cleansing started up, the most horrific example of which would be the massacre in Srebrenica. It was the Americans who, in 1995, forced peace upon the warring parties through the signing of the Dayton Agreement. But in 1998, the United States couldn't prevent war in Kosovo, which the Serbs sought to annex by force. I recall how, in 1999, on a ship from Venice to Turkey for the first leg of my Silk Road journey, I saw missiles being launched from NATO vessels.

Kosovo would proclaim its independence in 2008, preceded in 2006 by Montenegro. As we now cross the Balkan border, peaceful conditions prevail, tenuously maintained by UN armed forces.

*Slovenia (*Republika Slovenija*). Population: Two million, predominantly Catholic. Independence: 1991. Member of the European Union since 2004. A Eurozone nation. Capital city: Ljubljana.*

On our first day of hiking in the Balkans, we pass through the narrow strip of Slovenian territory that provides the country—squeezed between Italy, Croatia, Hungary, and Austria—with access to the sea. This "corridor" is so narrow that, setting out this morning from Trieste, we'll be in Croatia by evening, having crossed two borders in one day.

After the long Po Valley and its vast, flat rice paddies, rising before us is an immense geological fold that never stops until it's near the Black Sea. A succession of low, dry hills rises like a stairway. We opted for this more difficult route over the coastal road, which would have meant a long detour, and also, further north, the overcrowded road that Italians and Western Europeans take, drawn to Croatia's seemingly endless beaches. Though the route is direct, it's also quite strenuous, requiring us to heave Ulysses up the climbs and hold him back when descending. It's a good thing there's the two of us. We're changing countries, cultures, and altitudes. It's a lot for one day.

For our two border crossings, affable, good-humored customs agents keep formalities to a minimum. I even have to ask—or, more accurately, insist—to get them to stamp my passport: that's just how unconcerned the employees are upon seeing us, and they smile as they wave us across, without any further ado.

That's not how it is, though, for the Syrians, Afghans, and Palestinians who are traveling in the opposite direction, and whom Matteo and Cristina will take in—provided they're first able to get past the border crossings, that is. It's 2014, and the flow of arrivals is still nowhere near the full-fledged human tide that will, in another year, flow this way, and especially to Germany.

IX

CROATIA:
THE CROCODILE'S JAW

*Croatia (*Republika Hrvatska*). Population: 4.3 million, 89 percent Catholic. Serbian and Muslim minorities. Independence: 1991. Member of the European Union since 2013. Outside the Eurozone. Currency: the Croatian kuna. Capital city: Zagreb.*

As we prepare to set out on what is beyond a doubt the most difficult part of the journey, one question has me worried and I'm not alone: will Bénédicte's knee go the distance? And what about me? Will I have the energy to make it all the way to the Bosporus?

After a relatively short nineteen-mile journey, a picnic on the grass, and a second border crossing, I've burned through my last calorie. At 650 meters (2,100 feet), the temperature has plummeted, and though I slip on a sweater, I'm still shivering. In front of Jelovice's rustic church, a long rope attached to a tiny bell dangles the length of the facade to the ground. Directly across, the one and only inn is run by two colossal Serbs. The borscht they serve us, washed down with a sturdy local wine, puts an end to my shivers. Our contentment, though, is short-lived: after taking a shower, Bénédicte feels a sharp pain in her knee. If possible, we'll keep tomorrow's stretch down to a very short nine miles. Once we reach Rijeka, we'll have to talk. Three days off in Trieste was apparently not enough. As for me, that old cramp I get in my left thigh has flared up again, so I doubt that I'll be in any better shape than my partner. Still, our pains come on differently. Mine, with me as soon as I take my first steps, subsides after a few miles, right when hers is getting started. We are truly complementary.

We set out at 8:00 but have to stop walking around 1:00 in a tiny village: Bénédicte is in too much pain. What can we do? Rijeka is twelve or more miles away, much too far to travel with such throbbing pain. Luck is with us once again. A woman we ask for water discovers we're French. She calls to a little girl riding a bike in the yard, who looks to be about twelve. Her name is Sarah, and she comes over to us speaking our native tongue without the slightest accent. She was born in France to a Serbian father and a French mother, and, ever since the two separated, she comes here each summer to spend a few weeks with her father. Fully bilingual, Sarah leads the way to where we can catch a bus to Rijeka. She translates our request for the driver, who's willing to sell us two tickets but won't take euros. No worries, though: Sarah leads us straight to the post office where we can exchange our euros for local currency. Thank you, little lady!

Rijeka is long and narrow; looking out at the sea, it has its back against high hills. It's a historically important site. In 1920, the city, which has a long tradition of supercilious independence, became the Free State of Fiume, its Italian name. Inhabited by Hungarians, Croatians, and Italians, it held that status for only four years. The Kingdom of Yugoslavia annexed it but recognized that it deserved a certain degree of autonomy. In 1918, at the end of the war, US president Woodrow Wilson considered headquartering the League of Nations in Fiume, but, in the end, Geneva was chosen. Despite French and Italian protests, Tito annexed Fiume in no uncertain terms, which then lost its Italian name and took on a Croatian one, that of Rijeka.

In the bus taking us there, we imagined three possible solutions. If Bénédicte has only a simple case of tendonitis, we'll need a full week off. I'll continue on alone, and Bénédicte will take a train to meet up with me in Bihać, in Bosnia-Herzegovina. If she's advised to stop walking altogether, travel by bicycle might still be possible, in which case we'll buy a bike and keep on going, her on wheels and me on my feet. In the final scenario, if the injury is too serious, we'll head home. Bénédicte is shattered and I'm overcome with remorse. Given my experience, I ought to have shortened the first several stages between Verona and Padua. Getting lost on our way to see Giacomo only compounded that mistake. The first legs of extra-long journeys have to be short so that muscles aren't inundated with injury-causing toxins. To keep in shape, I first jog a little each morning, then do some stretching. It's a ritual I stuck to religiously in the days before our departure. Bénédicte, caught up in the hustle and bustle of the Avignon Festival, had no time whatsoever to prepare physically for the challenge ahead. Today, she's paying the price for her lack of conditioning . . . and my lack of good judgment.

The Youth Hostel we stay at is youthful in name only since it takes in old guys like me. Bénédicte tries to conceal her chagrin, but, for the first time in the six years we've been together, I catch a tear running down this tough woman's cheek. Since Italy, I've been calling her *minerale naturale* like the water we order with our meals, natural and full of minerals. She's a combination of strength and straightforward simplicity. She agrees not to take any unnecessary risks. How terrible we'd feel if, upon our return, she had to limp around while playing Suzanne in the *Marriage of Figaro*! I'm aware that Sarah Bernhardt wouldn't let a wooden leg keep her from performing, but Bénédicte, thankfully, hasn't got that famous actress's reputation to live up to.

A trip to the emergency room at Rijeka's hospital only half reassures us. The waiting room is a kind of *Cour des Miracles*, a hallway crowded with people. A stressed-out physician, a woman, diagnoses Bénédicte with tendonitis, then cuts the examination short when a blood-drenched girl is brought in on a stretcher. We don't insist. Bénédicte's injury is trivial as compared to what those here are dealing with.

I offer to spend the week off with her, but she dismisses the idea. The caravan must press on. Ilaria and Giacomo, who decided to come this way for a little Croatian beach hopping, tell us they'll be in the vicinity this afternoon. I'm too restless to wait. So that our team doesn't suffer a second injury, I've decided to take two days to travel from Rijeka to Crikvenica, whereas our travel schedule, drawn up in the coziness of our Norman home, had us doing it in just one. At 2:00 p.m., after glancing at the map, I decide to skip the coastal road and take the shortest route possible. Easier said than done, for it means I'll first have to attack a steep climb to the top of the little mountain the city backs up to. After only a few yards, I run into an obstacle: an overhanging road and a cliff. Determined to keep going, I try scaling it with Ulysses. Bénédicte, who has accompanied me this far, calls me crazy but gives me a boost. Perched atop the wall, I can then hoist my cart up behind me. I head off due north, toward the summit, after bidding my sweetheart a final farewell. I'm drenched in sweat; the slope is merciless. It's so steep in places that stairs have been carved into the rock and I get over each one by giving Ulysses's tow bar a violent jerk. When I reach a second staircase consisting of at least a hundred or more stairs, a man offers to lend me a hand. I finally reach the summit and turn east where, if I'm to believe my map, I should find the coastal road. But then, my morale takes a tumble, or rather, I almost go for a tumble myself. At my feet, plunging several hundred meters straight down, is an impossible cliff. In front of me, off in the distance down below, lies the road I was hoping to avoid. Obviously, there are no contour lines on my roadmaps, so I couldn't possibly have known that this barrier was here. Crushed, I retrace my steps and head back down the flight of stairs until I reach the youth hostel where I started. A two-hour struggle, all for nothing. I'd be tempted to go find Bénédicte and make the most of our young friends' visit, if it weren't for the Capricorn in me . . .

Down in the dumps, I head onto the coastal road with its furious engines. The coast is highly industrialized with an oil port and two shipyards, one for repairing ships and the other to build them. The view of the small islands is superb. Offshore, Krk Island (pronounced "kirk") is reached from the mainland by an elegant high suspension bridge. To my left, over by the cliff I ran into earlier, they put a highway and railroad through, either by having them run atop pylons or inside large chasms hewn into the rock.

Fed up with the endless line of cars, I notice a fig tree, heavy with perfectly ripe fruit, just off the road. I drop Ulysses's tow bar, jump to snag a branch, miss my target, trip on my cart on the way down, and tumble backwards onto the road where, by some miracle, there are no cars. I hit the ground hard and for a minute believe that I've either separated or dislocated my shoulder. Fortunately, the pain quickly subsides, and all I have to do is mop up the blood gushing from my injured elbow. It bleeds so heavily because I take a daily aspirin to head off a stroke. A few feet further, another fig tree, this time within reach, offers me a sweet feast, and I munch away with no hard feelings.

Around 5:00 p.m., having gone only 50 percent of the originally planned distance, I stop in the little village of Bakar. The only hotel is full. Afrim, a young, unscrupulous restaurant owner, tries to bamboozle me by putting me up for twice what a hotel room would cost—and in euros at that, which would be quite a killing. I laugh and cut the rate he's asking by three, which satisfies him just fine. In fact, he's so pleased with his sweetheart deal that he introduces me to his father, Nikola, who's surprised that a man my age—I'm ten years older—would risk such an adventure. It's true that, if he were to do like me, he'd lose his superb potbelly, which keeps him from seeing his feet.

My room has a magnificent view of the bay between Krk and the coast. I spend the evening revising our walking schedule. So far, we've added an extra week to our original plan. I identify all the stages over twenty-five miles and chop them in half. We won't be breaking any speed records. But if nothing else, I'd really like us to make it to the mythical city of Sarajevo.

In the morning, the bay is smooth as glass and athletes are out training on flimsy one- and two-person skiffs. Another longer boat has four rowers and a coxswain in it. The coaches follow behind on little motorboats and give their orders through megaphones. The place is so calm that if it weren't for an enormous cargo ship obscuring a large section of the island across the bay, one might easily mistake it for a Swiss lake. I take leave of Afrim and Nikola; they're both delighted by our encounter. The road winds to the top of a hill about three hundred meters high. The devil— speaking through Afrim—whispered to me that it would be crazy to ascend this high hill so early in the morning when there must be a passage along the coast, by way of the shipyard. The site's surrounded by high railings and is blocked by a metal barrier adorned with a sign, which I can reliably translate as "RESTRICTED AREA." A fifty-year-old Slav with a massive silhouette, prodigious belly, blue eyes, blond beard, and shaved head tells me to stop. I try chatting him up and, after a series of rebuffs, he eventually says, in perfect English: "Okay, but at your own risk." For the moment, the risks are minor: large puddles of black coal slurry, rails, and railcars waiting to be unloaded by huge cranes I have to pass beneath. I come to a railroad station and three employees, bored to tears. I expect they'll stop me, but they just sit there and let me go by. In fact, the one who looks to be their leader points me to an easy way through and teaches me how to pronounce "Crikvenica" in Croatian, which I immediately forget. I fear the gates will be closed. They're wide open. A little farther, a narrow road climbs off to my left and will perhaps take me to the state highway and a way forward. In reality, it leads to a builder's yard containing thirty or more huge steel vats. Large signs read "NO SMOKING." I've barely taken a few steps when a man spots me, jumps to his feet, and starts shouting at me in English. The place is extremely dangerous, full of explosive gases, and is strictly off limits. He clearly means business and so, pathetically, I turn around. I finally escape this industrial zone by clambering up a ditch topped with barbed wire. I find myself on a road leading to Bakarban, a five-house hamlet, three of which are restaurants. At the shore, makeshift diving boards have been improvised using utility poles set at forty-five-degree angles onto which planks have been nailed, providing access to a platform. Steel cables hold the structure in place.

I reach the road and descend into hell. A full-blown highway, it leads to the Krk Island bridge. The roadway has a strip about two feet across for a pedestrian, the width of Ulysses's wheels. I grow ever more nervous when a sidewall eliminates the pedestrian space. I forge ahead, ready at any moment to flatten myself against the wall, leaving my cart to its fate. After passing the turnoff to the island, I can breathe a bit. I realize a little too late that I actually missed the road to Crikvenica. Since I have no tolerance for turning back, I continue all the way around the bay, and estimate that what I thought was a shortcut has cost me at least six miles. The day's inventory of hardships would be incomplete if I failed to mention the storm battering the coast. I quickly cover Ulysses with a tarp. Passing cars blast me with road spray, and I have to tuck my head to avoid being blinded. A service station with an adjacent bar provides shelter from the storm, and for two hours, I watch the sky empty itself out over this supposedly idyllic coastline.

Crikvenica is a tourist-filled seaside resort. For fifty-five euros—an astronomical sum in this country—I get a room with a clogged sink and an uncomfortable bed. A quest for a ballpoint pen, mine having gone dry, forces me into a dozen shops selling hundreds of gadgets but no pens. The sky looks ominous: the crowd of vacationers has deserted the beach and is reveling in the joys of shopping. After an hour-long search, the only pen I come across is a promotional ballpoint with a little flag on the barrel that slowly disappears, revealing an advertisement for restaurants along the coast. It will run dry in two days. I dine beneath one of the tents set up between the nearby beach and the line of buildings. Since one of those always stimulating conversations with Bénédicte is out of the question, I set about organizing my notes and watch as the vacationers wander about. The women are pretty; almost all of them in light summer dress. Their clothing varies a great deal, as do their hairstyles. They're less influenced by magazines, which, in France, wind up making all women look alike.

The youngest walk with their mothers. The others, of which there are many, walk hand in hand with a boy. They flock around the ice cream vendors, apparently without any impact on their waistlines, but that's not the case for their mothers. Although there are Muslims in Croatia, other than a few grandmothers, I don't see any women with a scarf. What's most striking about the men is that they all wear size XXL: they have huge frames and potbellies to match. I do a quick count and find that about 60 percent of the men over thirty have spare tires, which they carry about with striking satisfaction. They walk arching their backs and swinging their arms to offset the excess weight. I see few obese young people. Another ballpark figure: about 40 percent of the men under twenty have shaved heads. At the hotel, I find an email in my inbox from Bénédicte, in a funk back at Rijeka's youth hostel. She sees her tendonitis as a personal failure. She thought she was stronger than that. I picture my Bénédicte—usually so mentally and physically on the go, incapable of sitting still for even five minutes—dreaming how one day, she'll be able to let loose. But she's making the most of this forced downtime by memorizing lines for the play she'll be performing in at the end of the summer. I liked it better when she rehearsed on the road.

In the night, an unusually strong storm strikes. Flashes of lightning illuminate the beach and one crash of thunder follows another. Before long, the power goes out. In the morning, the tourist machine is under water. The hotel's ground floor is now a lake, and the staff are busily trying to sweep it back out into the street. A full-fledged torrent gushes from a neighboring store: the water rushing down the hillside enters the building's rear and flows straight through. Employees watch on, resigned and powerless. Helpless owners in all the shops contemplate their floating merchandise. The very tourists out window-shopping yesterday, pleasantly surprised by this unexpected spectacle, parade by on a narrow median beyond the flood's reach and comment on all the damage. At the hotel, the guests—and in particular a group of retirees—anxiously wait, wondering whether the staff will be able to serve them their breakfast given that there's no electricity. "Not for at least another hour," someone tells them, though they've been waiting for two already. Thankfully, since Ulysses needed a minor repair, I carried all my camping gear up to my room last night. I would have found him under water in the TV room where he had been stowed. Since the manager can't run a credit card, he asks me to pay the fifty-five euros I owe him in cash. I hand him a one-hundred-euro note. He tries explaining that, in light of the situation, he had to raise rates, so he'll keep the entire thing. Nothing doing, I tell him, and he hands me my change.

On my way out of the city, I see a little pleasure boat which, carried by the flood, got stuck under a bridge, where it now lies half-submerged. Leaning over the bridge parapet, its desperate and helpless owner knows that he'll have to wait for the water to recede before he'll know how much damage there is. I climb halfway up the hill toward Route 8, whose dreadful traffic I'm all too familiar with, but what else can I do? The barometer is yo-yoing. A light breeze begins to blow, chasing away the clouds.

My optimism back with the good weather, I decide to skip the city of Povile where I was planning to spend the night. The landscapes are sumptuous; the hill falls steeply into the sea where rocks break through the surface. Across the way, Krk Island, stripped of vegetation, has assumed an earthy hue; I, on the other hand, so that motorists can see me, have donned a fluorescent orange T-shirt bought in Trieste, making me visible at a hundred yards. At noon, I reach the town of Novi Vinodolski. Cars have to slow down on their way through, resulting in a huge traffic jam and so, pulling Ulysses with a little provocative smile, I delightfully pass up the arrogant limousines that earlier had me shaking in my boots. Down by the little port, I lunch on a dish called "Etruscan Pasta," named for the ancient civilization that left us with some marvelous gold jewelry. Behind me, two young French show-offs flirt with our good-looking waitress, and she coos with pleasure. I take a nap down an inconspicuous path that opens out onto a beach made frothy by gentle waves. Not long after getting back on the road, I greet a Frenchman in a motorhome. He tells me he's crossed the whole country and has seen plenty of ruins.

That comes as no surprise, for I've read and heard the explanation why these vestiges of earlier acts of violence have been preserved. During Nazi occupation, many houses were burned in retaliation by the invaders. The inhabitants, instead of building new houses atop the old, preserved the ruins as poignant monuments to the tragedies they had suffered. And I later verify that the same thing was done in the aftermath of the Bosnian War: it's not uncommon to see a new house next to the ruins of one destroyed in the country's civil war, and a second set of ruins, attributable to the Nazis.

One of Ulysses's tires goes flat nine miles from Senj, where I was planning to spend the night. After patching the tire, I receive a long message from Bénédicte who does nothing to mask her distress. Inaction is eating away at her. She's full of doubts and cites Nicolas Bouvier's famous phrase, on which she has meditated at length: "You think you are making a trip, but soon it is making you—or un-making you."* I try reassuring her. "It's not true, *ma chérie*, you have not been 'unmade'—only delayed! In setting out, we think we're strong. On the road, we find out just how strong we really are. We get the measure of a journey over the duration, not after one misadventure. And since when do trials unmake a person? My own experience, on the contrary, has shown me that they make us stronger." Bénédicte will overcome this, and I rather boldly assure her: "We will set foot into Sarajevo together, your hand in mine!"

On August 22, at 11:00 a.m., I arrive in Senj, relieved to have finally left the Croatian coast behind. I can't bear any more souvenir shops or aggressive billboards touting brands great only in terms of the advertising budgets behind them; I've had my fill of tattoos and tattooed people, of the smell of gas and burnt diesel. After this city, my

---

* Nicolas Bouvier. *The Way of the World*. Marlboro Press, 1992, translated by Robyn Marsack, 16. Originally self-published in 1963 as *L'usage du monde*.

route veers directly east. There, I hope to find a little more authenticity and meet more people. I meet back up with Bénédicte as well, who gets here from Rijeka by bus, and who will leave again tomorrow for Bihać in Bosnia-Herzegovina, where she'll wait up for me. Her spirits have improved and she's no longer in pain, but she won't start walking again until after this weekend, which we've set aside for rest.

We're roused from our slumber by the thunder of a storm beating down on the city. I sluggishly get myself ready, but then, since the rain fails to let up, I decide to brave the deluge. Bénédicte accompanies me downtown where we sip a hot beverage, for the temperature has plummeted; then it's time to part ways once more. Thinking back, it's probably this difficult farewell that caused me to drop my guard yet again. I head out into heavy traffic, showered by each passing car. The surroundings have changed. Gone are the flat little seaside roads. Yesterday evening, I saw on the map that I'll be passing near summits over a thousand meters high. I'm truly entering the Balkan Mountains. After an hour-and-a-half climb made all the more grueling with Ulysses wrenching my arms out of their sockets, I come to a three-road intersection but not a single sign. A man, who introduces himself as a soldier, tells me that I'm not on the road to Bihać at all, but that I'm headed to Zagreb, Croatia's capital: it's to the northeast, whereas Bihać is to the east. My first reaction, as always, is to keep on going. I hate doubling back. Am I unable to accept that I made a mistake? Is it out-of-place vanity making me believe that to turn around is to lose, or is it just laziness, since my mistake means I have even farther to go? One thing's for sure: when I walk, I never want to see the same stretch of road twice. So I'm pushing on, I tell him, but the soldier's categorical: if I go from village to village, I'm sure to get lost, for I'll wind up in some forest with nothing to point me in the right direction. He ushers me into a nearby bar and the customers launch into a group discussion, each one explaining what I need to do . . . in Serbo-Croatian, which doesn't do me much good. Finally, with a heavy heart, I give in and turn around; I make my way back to Bénédicte, who, though she feels bad for me, is delighted we've gained an extra afternoon together.

Children, in this country, are truly venerated. Parents and grandparents take turns caring for them. It occurs to me that the situation here is like that of France after the war. In the late 1940s and especially in the '50s, the French indulged in two passions: childbearing and the domestic arts. The consumer cravings I've observed here would seem to confirm this. Do consumer goods and children soften the memory of hardships endured?

I consult the map, but carefully this time. If I go by way of Otočac, I'll have to cover seventy-three miles in three days. That's a lot, but I'm up to it given the shape I'm in at this point. I once again bid Bénédicte farewell. See you three days from now in Bihać, where I'll be by late afternoon. Today, August 23, I'm up at 6:00. I want to tackle the uphill stretch during the cool hours, those best for walking. Traffic is light and, instead of the stench of diesel and gasoline I've had to cope with over the past few days, there's the delightful fragrance of wild thyme, which grows abundantly here. A little after leaving Senj, I pass a cemetery that, wedged inside the narrow valley, rises in terraces for at least five hundred yards. Croats spare no expense when it comes to honoring their dead. The gravestones are imposing and are often made of black granite. There's a diversity of religious symbols. Many drivers hang rosaries with cross pendants from their rearview mirrors.

By 9:00 a.m., I've climbed 310 meters (1,020 feet), having calibrated my altimeter at sea-level yesterday afternoon. I take a cookie-and-banana break, then, in a restaurant I discover immediately thereafter, I treat myself to a cappuccino. I had resolved to drink less coffee, but here I am, practically an addict. Out in the middle of nowhere is a monumental fountain dedicated to Ferdinand I of Austria. An onion-domed chapel adjoins it. At 11:00, after a four-hour climb, I reach the pass, which my altimeter-barometer-chronometer-thermometer-compass tells me is at seven hundred meters (2,300 feet). Probably erected for defensive purposes, a small building equipped with arrow slits is slowly giving way to the hands of time.

Heading down the other side, I finally glimpse the Croatian back-country. People have begun to rebuild. Many hollow-brick houses are unfinished. One or two have walls that were begun, but then abandoned, halfway up. Exhausted after a twenty-five-mile journey and numerous climbs up steep slopes, I reach Otočac and rent a room in the hotel-restaurant. Two charming and chatty waitresses inform me, in English, that there's a small road I can take tomorrow. The next morning, as I'm saying goodbye, they pull from the counter a large sandwich and a piece of fruit, prepared just for me, for which they refuse to take even a single kuna, Croatia's currency.

Outside town, the landscape is rather dreary. Vast fields lie fallow, as if the country's farmers had given up cultivating them. By the side of the road, two young Germans on their way to Albania, who spent the night in their car, invite me to join them for a cup of tea. By 11:00, I've gone through all my water. I hold out my empty canteen to a man working in his garden. He's huge, like all Slavs. I use every Croatian word I know: *"Dobar dan! Voda, molim vas?"* (Good day to you! Water, please?), and I prepare my *"hvala"* (thank you) which usually comes after, but, with an annoyed gesture, the fellow invites me to go do my begging somewhere else. It's the second time in all my nomadic existence that I'm refused water. The first was on a farm in the Pyrenees, despite being listed as an official mountain refuge by the FNRP, the French Hiking Federation.* Only those renting the gîte were allowed to drink their water. So let the poor die (of thirst)! As it turned out, I had to rescue a group of penniless young people who, like me, hadn't been allowed to refill their jugs at the gîte. They ran out of water on a difficult portion of the trail, and one young woman in their group was on the verge of passing out. I gave them the water I had and later wrote to the FNRP asking that the gîte be removed from its list.

---

* TN: The *Fédération française de randonnée pédestre (FFRandonnée).*

A little farther along, an old woman behind an iron gate is pushing an electric mower over her yard's postage-stamp lawn:

"*Dobar dan! Voda, molim vas?*"

She stops the machine, opens the gate, and points me to a faucet above a steel sink. As I'm filling up on water, in a hodgepodge of German, English, and Croatian, she asks—of course—where I'm from and where I'm going.

"French?" She throws me a broad smile. "*Kava?*"

"Gladly!"

She vanishes into the house, then steps back out along with a short, stocky, friendly faced fellow who thrusts his hand in my direction and introduces himself: Nikola. While his spouse prepares the coffee, he shows me a pen where he raises giant rabbits. The mama doe weighs eleven pounds. He rears chickens, too, and a couple sheep. He speaks English quite well and, when Lumturi, his wife, arrives with the coffee, we settle into a comfortable spot in the shade and revel in the pleasures of the encounter. Seventy-year-old Nikola is Croatian; he was a telecom engineer before retiring. Sixty-nine-year-old Lumturi is Albanian and was a teacher. They have three children: two boys who work in Senj, and a daughter in Zagreb, the mother of a little boy. It's time for me to shove off again but, as I'm getting ready, they do a quick consultation, then invite me to join them for lunch. I gladly accept. Offering someone a glass of water or a cup of coffee is an act of generosity but offering a meal is something entirely different. It's not simply opening one's door; it's inviting others into one's world. It demonstrates a willingness to take the exchange further, for the sharing of food opens not only appetites, but hearts as well.

With Lumturi busy at work in the kitchen, Nikola shows me around the little workshop he set up in a corner of their yard. He proudly shows me the oven he built and its rotating spit, activated by a recycled washing machine motor. I burst out laughing, for I, too, upcycled an old washing machine motor, only in my case, it was to power a grinder so I could sharpen my tools. I really like a fellow who cares enough about his objects to want to give them a second life.

When the meal's ready, I prepare to take off my shoes before stepping into their house, as is the custom here, but Nikola won't let me. We sit down in an attractive living room. They turn on the television, which is their way of honoring me. They bombard me with questions and, since their English only goes so far, we finish our sentences with animated gestures. They're on cloud nine. Lumturi has the smile of a little girl, and her entire being radiates great kindness. Nikola knows three French words, and proudly instructs me: *"Asseyez-vous"* (Sit down). He then asks me if I'm on YouTube. I haven't the slightest clue. He switches on his computer and types my name. To my great surprise, I discover a whole slew of video shorts, probably taken from televised interviews, and I'm shocked to see that there are even a few clips from films I took myself and which somehow found their way onto the internet, I have no idea how.

Lumturi sets the dishes out on the table: chicken, sausages, red beets, fries, cucumbers, and a cake; that's on top of the unavoidable *börek*, those little stuffed triangles I love. To my great surprise, there are only two sets of utensils. I suggest that Lumturi should eat with us, but the two refuse and my hostess plops herself down in an armchair to watch her favorite Turkish soap opera. We discuss the weather, the coming autumn, and, above all, what winter's like here. As early as November, snow begins to fall and paralyzes the country. Nikola showed me his enormous woodpile and the huge shovels he uses to clear pathways between their house and the outbuildings. I get back underway, overjoyed at having met these people, deeply moved by their hospitality, generosity, and nobility of heart. They will be my best Croatian memory. When I take leave of them, they hug me as if I were their son, even though they're eight years younger than me. I have been adopted.

Vrhovine is a large market town whose uppermost house sits 750 meters (2,500 feet) above sea level. A monument lists the names of 133 people killed in 1944 by *"fašističkog terora"* (fascist terror). Soon after, I enter Plitvice Lakes National Park, a UNESCO World Heritage site, which encompasses a winter sports complex. I veer off the highway and head into the forest on a narrow road where I'll more likely encounter a bear than a truck. There's a winding mountain stream, and the gentle music it produces is more pleasant than the roaring engines out on the main road. I can finally breathe. At a bend in the road, I behold a marvelous work of art: a gorgeous forest house that, as an avid do-it-yourselfer, I examine from every angle. The woodwork has been carefully assembled and is held together by pegs. I'd be willing to bet that there isn't a single nail in the entire structure. The roof is made of chestnut shakes—split from the log, not sawed—which work just as well as slate shingles.

Plitvički Ljeskovac is a tiny hamlet deep in the forest. I count fewer than a half-dozen fully intact houses, and nearly as many in ruins, located on either side of the little river I've been following. It's 5:30 p.m., I've been walking since morning, and I really want to get near the Bosnian border as quickly as possible. I have to be careful, though, not to get lost in the forest as darkness falls. A family is enjoying the cool air out in front of their house. Sonja, a young woman who speaks perfect English, translates for me her parents' directions as to the route I need to take. The next hotel is six miles away and, they tell me, it's currently completely booked. So I opt to be safe rather than sorry. They offer—"for free," they insist—a spot in the adjacent field where I can pitch my tent. That done and having dined on some of the food I brought with me, I chat with Sonja. I ask her about the dozens of abandoned houses in the village. Over the past two days, I've seen them everywhere. Some are half-collapsed. Sonja explains that, paradoxically, it wasn't armed conflict that created these ruins, but fear. As the threat of war grew between the Yugoslavian Army (consisting primarily of Serbs) and the Croatian Army, residents were told by those on both sides that they should leave, or risk being killed. A mass exodus emptied the villages, and the deserted houses were soon looted. Many emigrants headed to the European Union and the United States. Few ever returned. A small number of couples, whose houses weren't destroyed, still come back to spend their holidays here, but their children have definitively turned the page and put the country of their birth out of their minds. For those who remained behind like Sonja, who's pursuing a degree in environmental studies, there was hardly any other alternative than to move to the city or go into exile with families that had already settled abroad, for unemployment is high here.

At daybreak, I leave Plitvički Ljeskovac, its empty houses, and the little mountain stream that sang to me all night long. Crossing the forest is sheer bliss. It's a cathedral of immense beech trees, some of which must soar a hundred feet into the air. This forest, apparently, hasn't been logged since the war that resulted in Croatia's creation— for the past twenty-three years, that is. The road, which occasionally is but a simple stone path, climbs steeply in short switchbacks. The soft morning light, filtered through the beech leaves high overhead, takes my mind off the freezing night, and how the walls of my tent were soaked on the outside from morning dew and on the inside from condensation. In a bistro where I'm hoping to find something to eat after twelve miles on an empty stomach, all they can serve me is . . . a cup of coffee.

I'll just have to hope I find something at the border, but there again, no dice. The customs post is a very elegant, aerial steel structure anchored by wires. Beneath the huge, curved roof, the two facilities—one Croatian, one Bosnian—stand sixty feet apart; the agents are located inside windowed guard booths, like those seen at highway toll plazas. The Croatian customs officer is a delightful, smiling, blond-haired woman; but the Bosnian policeman has all the looks and amiability of a bear. He growls as he stamps my passport and pretends not to have heard my greeting in English, so he doesn't have to reply.

I'm entering Bosnia-Herzegovina, the Balkan nation where the very worst atrocities took place, as well as that horrific practice known as ethnic cleansing.

* * *

Jajce, Central Bosnia—September 2

Surprise number one: Bosnia is France's Auvergne region in the Orient. In a magnificent landscape of forest-covered highlands, minarets shoot toward the sky alongside orthodox onion domes and Catholic bell towers.

Surprise number two: the bullet and artillery holes that look as fresh as if they'd been made yesterday; the collapsed balconies disfiguring the facades of countless buildings in cities and villages.

Surprise number three on the road to Sarajevo we've been traveling for the past five days: signs warning of land mines, memorials commemorating the wars of 1940 and 1992, and houses in ruins, which probably caught fire when struck by grenades. Beside each is a new, hastily built house of lightweight, uncoated brick. Are these gifts from the European Union, offered to make people forget its impuissance?

The road is a bit like a cemetery, but with landscapes so beautiful they sometimes make us forget that, twenty years later, war is still quite near.

The night sky—unbelievably clear in these regions where, for three days now, we haven't seen a single soul except in cars—offers us the breathtaking spectacle of hundreds of constellations. It's one of the gifts of camping, when you reluctantly decide to climb out of your bedroll and go for a pee. But you never linger long: it's freezing cold beneath the stars!

Our inability to speak the language keeps us from conversing with farmers and shepherds, but the sincere, broad, and joyful smiles that return our salutations of "dobar dan" (good day) delight us, as do blasts from truck drivers' horns, whether meant to encourage us, or to express how surprised they are to see our odd-looking buggy. In town, we make do by speaking a mishmash of German, English, and a sprinkling of Serbo-Bosno-Croatian words picked up along the way. The inhabitants of this little country, torn between three religions and three cultures, are delightful. But wariness is still the order of the day. We'd be wary too, after three years of war. When we ask for water to refill our jugs, people leave us waiting on the doorstep; but then, when we head off again, their eyes remain with us for a very long time!

The men's faces here are full of character: sullen, folded, flattened, square, stubbly, gruff-looking, chubby. They have noses like drainpipes and chins like parapets. One could sketch a thousand portraits.

As for the women, they're tall and slender, the exception being farm workers whose sturdy physiques are the result of working hard out in the fields, where even today they gather hay with wooden pitchforks.

Many of the younger women, whose long hair is rarely tied back, have stunning legs with matching rears, tightly stuffed into faded jeans. They're courteous and shy. What do they dream about?

The nice surprise here is just how little traffic there is. We feel safe. But since improvising our way forward is out of the question given all the landmines still lying about, and since the roads on Google Maps (you heard right: can anyone manage without Google?) occasionally turn out to be just bramble-filled pathways, we don't even bother looking for shortcuts the way Bernard likes to do, we stick to the main road.

It has been raining since sun-up on September 1, and the tempera-ture has dropped from the mid-eighties to the mid-fifties. There's a little something for everyone!

The tendinitis in my knee—which forced me, with heavy heart, to stop for a week in Rijeka while Bernard zipped along from city to city—still has me hobbling. The pain returns after about twelve miles. It's discour-aging, but I've resolved to just push right on through. The tactic seems to be working. But at a pace I can manage, Istanbul is still a long way off! We nevertheless decide to shorten the stages.

As for Bernard, he's plugging along like the young man he still is, though an ache in his left hip, which he treats with contempt, occasion-ally reminds him it's still there. What a marvelous man! I already knew that—and of course, you did too—but now I know for sure, so I'll say it once again! It will be six years tomorrow since we first met along the banks of the Loire, and it's as if he had just climbed out of his canoe, shivering and smiling.

The ordeal of life on the road (for it's that, too) is bringing us closer together than ever before.

See you next in Sarajevo!
BF

X

LANDMINES AHEAD!

*Bosnia-Herzegovina (*Bosna i Hercegovina*). Population: 3.8 million. 46 percent Muslim (Bosniak*), 36 percent Orthodox, and 15 percent Catholic. Independence: 1995 (Dayton Agreement). Outside the European Union and Eurozone. Currency: the convertible mark (*konvertibilna marka*). Capital city: Sarajevo.*

It's only three miles beyond the border that I simultaneously spot a restaurant sign and the first minaret, thin as a needle, equipped with the customary loudspeakers—so the muezzin can give the call to prayer five times a day without climbing to the top. My belly full, fatigue gets the best of me. I really need to take a break and dry my camping gear, which has been soaked and stewing inside its stuff sack since morning. On a hillside, I spread out my tent and sleeping bag liner, then try, to no avail—too much tension, too much exhaustion—to catch a few Zs. When I get back underway, determined to make my destination before nightfall, I walk at over four miles per hour. I'm stopped three or four times by friendly bystanders wanting to know where I'm from and where I'm going. When I finally reach Bihać, bone-tired after eleven hours of walking, over twenty-five miles, and three mountain passes all in one day, I think to myself how it would be a good idea if, every now and then, I kept in mind

---

* Bosnian: an inhabitant of Bosnia-Herzegovina, regardless of religion. Bosniak: a term typically used to refer to a Muslim inhabitant of Bosnia-Herzegovina only.

that I'm seventy-six! While walking toward Bihać's *most* (bridge) where I'm supposed to meet up with Bénédicte, I suddenly hear her voice from the opposite sidewalk. She came to meet me. Pure joy. We embrace as one. She immediately tells me that she wants to get back on the road, and whatever happens happens. She's fed up with just sitting around. But she'll have to hold on for another twenty-four hours, since it's my turn to recharge my batteries now, especially since that old pain in my left thigh has flared up again, to such an extent that I had to stop several times to do some stretching.

She rented a room from an extremely considerate old lady who, the moment I arrive, invites us for coffee and *bosanski uštipci* (Bosnian donuts). She does so again the following day, but then, as we ready to depart, she hands us a bill for "the many little extras," which gives us a good chuckle. Nothing's free, especially for supposedly filthy-rich Westerners. We catch a concert that evening at the 2014 Bihać Festival. It has a distinctive local flavor: before the concert, all the town's political figures hold forth for an hour. We of course catch nothing. The drone of the seven accordions lined up at the front of the grandstand is so loud that the strings behind them can't be heard. Five or six singers perform, one after the other. They're all over forty and two are in their sixties. Which is in keeping with the audience: compared to my neighbors, I look like a young man. There are no teenagers here. We'll spot them later out in the streets, on the way back to our host's house.

Bihać, which is 60 percent Muslim, has a reputation for resistance, come what may. In 1878, the Austro-Hungarians had to keep up their siege of the city for nearly a month to get it to finally surrender. In World War II, the "Bihać Republic" again offered stiff resistance to German and Italian occupying forces from November 1942 to January 1943. When "ethnic cleansing" was being carried out, the Bihać pocket, in which nearly two hundred thousand Muslims found refuge, held strong against the Serbs' attacks. A Croatian Army offensive, launched to rescue the beleaguered population, finally loosened the Serbian noose. We're rather surprised to see so many mosques, proof of a large Muslim presence, but out in the street, how could anyone tell Muslims from the city's other inhabitants? How could a Serbian, Croat, or Bosnian sniper be sure who it was he had in his sights before pulling the trigger? How could two neighbors kill one another, even though they probably shared common ancestors, one of the two having simply converted? And conversions took place in both directions, according to whether the occupying army happened to be for the Cross or for the Crescent, with, at times, yet another change of religion when some new conqueror-prince would impose his.

What we set out on today, August 28, is nothing short of a senior stroll. Last night, poring over our pitiful map, we cut the Bihać–Bosanski Petrovac stretch in half. We'll spend the night in Lipa, a tiny village eleven miles away. Wary of my inclination to walk too fast, I ask Bénédicte to lead the way on condition that, if her knee starts to hurt, she'll either slow down or stop.

Death is all around. In one hamlet we come to, near a bullet-ridden house, a small monument reads: 1992–twelve killed; 1993–three killed; 1994–two killed. All the first names are Muslim. In 1996–five killed, including three women. And yet it was in December 1995 that the Dayton Agreement was signed, imposing peace.

Six miles after setting out, we noticed a small road on our map that offers an attractive shortcut to Lipa. We take it, our hearts light. Though narrow, it's a decent paved road, free of houses. We walk happily along, sharing discoveries made during our involuntary separation. Only twice does a truck force us off the road and onto the shoulder. After two or three miles, we start to smell a terrible stench. It's coming from a huge, open-air dump, surrounded by barbed wire. It's home to dozens of dogs that feed off the garbage. Puppies come running over to us, hoping we'll either pet them or offer them something to eat. We pick up the pace until we can breathe again. The road is soon no more than a stony path; it then turns grassy and splits in two, one branch veering north, the other east. I take the path to our right. According to my map once again, it ought to put us on a back road to Lipa, our destination. After a few hundred yards, it becomes barely passable, given how thick the vegetation is. Then, suddenly, I panic: hundreds of acres in Bosnia are strewn with landmines and earlier we saw several signs warning of them. During the war, the front lines were packed solid with these deadly devices. If a route on my map is no longer visible in the field, it might well be because it's full of mines. What I've started out on here is sheer madness. And yet, I carefully read all the guidebooks, which strongly recommend that travelers never wander off-road, unless the local population tells them it's okay to do so. We're in the backwoods, where no one can advise us. I turn to Bénédicte and, trying to hide my alarm, order her—in a tone she'll later tell me she found unusual—to walk behind me, staying a good distance back, at least sixty feet. She seems confused by what I'm saying but complies. I press on, increasingly anxious, expecting with each step to be ripped apart by an anti-personnel mine. I foolishly keep going, driven by my stubborn distaste for doubling back, hoping to find a path that will lead us back to the road. In the end, the vegetation decides for me: the path completely disappears, there's no telling which way to go. We have no choice but to swallow our pride, turn around, and head back to the main road. I stop, paralyzed by fear and anger. I turn to Bénédicte:

"We have to go back to the fork in the road. Whatever the map says, this is a dead end."

"Just how far have we gone down this lovely shortcut?"

"Two and a half, perhaps three miles. And we'll have traveled it twice."

So instead of eleven miles, we'll have gone seventeen. That's one hell of a short stage. But who could've known? The map is perfectly unambiguous; on paper, the road is clearly marked!

"By the way," my wife asks a little later on, "why did you have me walk so far behind you? That's not something you usually do when were not on a road . . ."

"A little late, it suddenly occurred to me there might be landmines. No point in both of us losing a leg."

"What?! You were thinking of dying alone? But we agreed that we'd either die together or not at all! Promise me you'll never forget that again."

"Yes, it slipped my mind. I promise."

In Dubovsko, where there's not a soul in sight, we set up our tent behind an unfinished house, but not before first checking to be sure that the awning we're planning to sleep under isn't booby-trapped. We avoid going inside: many abandoned houses are mined. After nightfall, this far from electric lighting and at such high elevation, the sky puts on a magical display of constellations.

Vrtoče is a real-life replica of a traditional village. People have told us good things about it and have assured us that it's so large and hospitable that we'll have no trouble finding a bed there. It consists of small cabins scattered about a wooded area. In the middle is a traditional house with a cut-stone ground floor. The second floor is a large, rectangular room lit by twenty-four windows, six to a wall. It's the "masonry-tent" concept I often found in Asia, in central Turkey in particular. Unfortunately, everything is booked solid. I joke with Ermina, an employee who speaks rather good English, and try to convince her that there's simply no way we can go any farther. As we feared, our two afflictions have flared up again, and we've arrived here in rather poor shape. Ermina promises to try to work something out and, a half hour later, she's back, along with a young man whom she introduces: he's David, the owners' son. His parents gifted him a house, a beautiful little log cabin tucked away beneath the trees. It's a mortise-and-tenon-joint structure, the same technique the pioneers of the American West used when the only tool they had for building their houses was an axe. David's happy to rent us his personal palace for ten euros a night, a rate negotiated by Ermina. So we settle into the cabin, which measures about sixteen feet by nine. The meal that evening consists primarily of grilled meats. Bosnia is one gigantic barbecue grill, and on it sizzles either a sheep or a pig, depending

on whether the region you're in is Muslim or Christian. There are
very few vegetables and no soups. It's not the most suitable diet for
walkers, but we make do.

While we're seated at table, a man comes over and asks us: "Are
you French?" Zukic is quite fluent in our native tongue but has
a strong accent. He's delighted to meet us and tells us his story.
As a young man, he emigrated to the city of Nantes for work.
There, he pursued a career. He had no trouble integrating into
the community and, he says, was well-liked at the firm where he
worked. He married a French woman, and they had two daughters whom he goes to see from time to time. When he finally
retired, he returned to his home village where he came to a quick
realization: in France he would be a modest retiree with limited
means, but here, given the large disparity in exchange rates, he
could live it up. Divorced from his French wife, he lives with a
Bosnian woman.

Getting back underway, we walk slowly, for we're both gimping
a bit. The countryside is magnificent. Vast forests, rolling hills. The
first few yellowing leaves already signal autumn's arrival. Bénédicte,
who's walking ahead of me while reading aloud her lines in the
play, suddenly interrupts what she's doing, stops, turns around, and,
between fear and hope, asks: "Do you really think we'll make it to
Istanbul?" How do I answer that? When I walked alone, I never
asked myself that kind of question, except one day when, in the
Gobi Desert, I decided to throw in the towel after receiving some
bad news from Seuil.* In the morning, my energy had returned, and
I kept on going. But what about today? It's clear that, when there are
two walkers instead of one, the risk of giving up is twice as great.
And I sense that Bénédicte is starting to worry, fearing that she's the

---

* TN: The Seuil Association's first accompanied walk was underway (see the description of Seuil at the end of this book). The two teenage participants had run into serious
trouble. The event is described in volume two of this series, *Walking to Samarkand*,
Part II, Chapter VIII: "Depression."

lead weight that might prevent me, the veteran walker, from making it to the finish line. She's wrong. I've resolved that, if she has to stop again, I'll stop, too. After all, I'm much less motivated than her. It's she who dreamt of embarking on this journey with the man she loves, and who made me want to get back on the road. It's a desire I would not have had on my own: as far as walking is concerned, I have nothing more to prove. Moreover, even though my love for Bénédicte is total and I'm happy for her happiness, two-person journeys are not my cup of tea. Not until much later did I tell the love of my life how I reveled in walking alone during her forced week off. I rediscovered the feelings and delights that carried me first to Compostela, then to Xi'an, fifteen years ago. And I saw once again how traveling alone increases the likelihood of meeting people, such as Nikola and Lumturi. I love those moments of mutual attraction in which souls embrace, when new friendships—if only for a day, and perhaps precisely because it's only for a day—become the journey's driving force. Since Lyon, I've had confirmation that, when you're traveling as a couple, connecting with local populations is next to impossible. But we're partly to blame, too. We didn't take time to learn the languages of the countries we're traveling through. Inspired by bits and pieces of vocabulary gleaned from travel guides, such as *Is the street noisy at night?* or *Where can I find a gas station?*, Bénédicte has done most of the talking. As for me, gifted with a lousy memory, which age has not made any better, I've been limited to conversing with English- or French-speakers. The smattering of Spanish I speak is of no use here.

But Bénédicte is not alone in worrying about her health. Will I myself be able to mobilize my body and my energy? From the moment we left Lyon, I've noticed a clear decline in my own physical abilities as compared to when I was in my sixties. Recovery times are longer now, and the pain in my left thigh never lets up, whereas back then, it always went away after a few days. The stretches of twenty-two to twenty-five miles I walked to meet back up with Bénédicte completely wore me out, whereas, on the roads of Asia, I traveled at least that distance every single day. And, as each afternoon draws to a close, I dream of sleeping in a bed rather than a tent. I've slowed down and gone soft.

Will I—will we—make it to the finish line? I still have no clue.

XI

THE BALKANS: AFTER THE HATRED

Can Western Europe—our home—bring prosperity and happiness to the peoples of the Balkans, who have suffered so much from war, religious intolerance, and poverty? It's still an open question after our first month on the road. Yes, houses are being repaired and signs have been posted here and there, making it known that the European Union and international organizations like Caritas fronted the money to rebuild them. But what about that little extra heart and soul? What about political will? The European Union didn't exactly distinguish itself in the atrocious war that took place here. What did it do to stop that gruesome policy of ethnic cleansing, whose countless victims lie in Christian and Muslim tombs all along our route? It took the determination of the United States, the Dayton Agreement, and the military might of NATO to restore peace in the region. Europe played a secondary role at best. This is proof that, so long as European unity is based only in commercialism, free markets, and to some extent monetary policy, it will remain powerless to stamp out conflict and defuse hatred. Money has never brought people together. Quite the opposite: it most often gives rise to discord. The solution will only come about through real political union, and education.

Yes, people are free to travel both within and among these countries. But just because a country joins the European Union doesn't mean all barriers will simply fall away. Language, culture, religion, and customs are obstacles too, and they remain. Feelings of hatred live on. Especially since everyone knows today that the Croatian and Serbian armies spent less time fighting one another than they did attacking unarmed civilian populations. The region had to be "cleansed." Excuses do not efface overnight how souls and bodies have been torn apart.

Today, the 31st of August, we'll have walked twenty-five and a half miles for a stretch that our maps told us was twenty-two. In a meadow overlooking a valley near the border with the Republika Srpska, a picnic-plus-siesta perks us up. Bénédicte, markedly limping, finds it hard to get going again; her inflamed knee is very painful. She asks me to whittle a branch into a walking stick for her and, leaning on it, finishes the day's journey. In adjacent fields all along the road, farmers are cutting grass with scythes, then piling it into haystacks kept upright by a pole planted in their middle.

In Ključ, we look for the Red Apple Inn, which Zukic, the Bosnian from Nantes, recommended. But it either doesn't exist or has closed. After wandering about for a while, a visibly tipsy fellow staggers over to us. We manage to communicate in a joyful jumble of German and Serbo-Croatian. He invites us to *"Komm mit mir."* With him unsteady on his feet from alcohol, and us from excessive fatigue, we make an odd-looking trio, but off we go, swaying our way to the bus station. He introduces us to a charming receptionist who rents us a small apartment. She has an adorable, child-like smile. She speaks fluent German, which she picked up in Switzerland where she had been sent for her safety, just like many other kids whose parents wanted to save them from the atrocities of civil war. During this terrible time, several European countries took in scores of refugees, children and adults from the Balkans.

Considering Bénédicte's knee, I decide that we'll travel tomorrow's stage by bus, and that this time, we'll stick together. I'm not about to go it alone again. This morning, on the square beside the bus station, there are plenty of teenagers. It's back-to-school. The girls are striking with bright green or blue eyes, and the boys are almost all sporting the latest hairstyle: shaved sides and a thick mop on top. Once again, I find myself wondering how anyone could ever tell Muslim Bosniaks from Christian Bosnians. There is no overt sign of religious affiliation on any of these kids. And fashion, that steamroller of individuality, has them all looking more or less the same. It's the immense Muslim cemetery that tells us that a large majority here believes in Allah.

The weather and Bénédicte approve of this little breach in protocol. No sooner has the bus left the city than a driving rain obscures the countryside. The road climbs to over eight hundred meters (2,600 feet), and I imagine we would have faced at least a three-hour footslog in a torrential, icy rain.

At Jajce, the Kod Asima restaurant is nestled inside a traditional house boasting beautiful wooden decor. Hardly adventuresome where food is concerned, I opt for the goulash, while Bénédicte points a hungry finger to a dish on the menu she knows nothing about. *Bajanki Lonak* is a delicious meat-and-vegetable stew served in a clay bowl. We round off our meal with a honey-rich slice of baklava. Outside, the sky has opened up. Instead of spending the night cold and wet in our tent, we sleep warm and dry in a youth hostel by the banks of the Pliva, the river that runs through this market town. A short distance downstream, it spills into the Vrbas in a series of spectacular waterfalls a hundred feet high, in the very heart of town. The next day, the showers haven't let up. We decide to bus it to Travnik rather than face twenty-eight miles in the pouring rain. Brazenly dishonest, I explain to Bénédicte that, since there's no lodging anywhere in between, we'd have a tough time caring for our tendonitis in a tent.

We greedily savor the joys of being far from everyday household concerns. Here, there's no international news. We don't understand a thing on the TV sets we find in every restaurant, except that the weather in France this August is no better than here. Since, to our great surprise, Wi-Fi is free and readily available wherever we go, I keep abreast of world events on my phone. There's been a change of government in France, a referendum has been scheduled in Scotland,* and, sadly, war has broken out in Iraq and especially Syria. How fortunate we were to be able to walk in the eastern part of that marvelous country in 2010. We wistfully recall the kindness and wonderful hospitality the Syrians showed us, even though we were there during Ramadan; but today, the news speaks only of the savagery of war. With this one terrifying question: what has become of the people we met?

Prior to the Ottoman conquest, Jajce and Travnik were large cities. Then the Austro-Hungarians occupied the territory. Each army, of course, did what it could to impose its religion. After World War I, Travnik regained prominence, but then World War II brought its share of deaths. Tito, at the head of the anti-Nazi resistance, resided here briefly in 1943. When Yugoslavia broke apart, there were as many Muslims in the city as Bosnian Croats, as well as a minority of Bosnian Serbs. Then ethnic war began to rage. To which bullet-riddled house facades still bear witness. Downtown, a war memorial located in the shadow of a mosque lists over two hundred Christian names for the years 1992 and 1993 alone. After the war, the Bosnian Serbs left. Only those who died remain. We find three cemeteries in the city, two Muslim and one Christian.

Today, September 3, would be a day just like any other if, in 2008, chilled to the bone as I stepped out of my canoe halfway through a paddle down the Loire River, I had not met Bénédicte.† Like so many others, she had offered to put me up. Less than a year later, she was moving to Normandy to share in my life and live in my house. For the past six years, our love has been serene, strong, and free of

---

* TN: The fourth change of government under President François Hollande was finalized on August 26, 2014, and is referred to as the second *gouvernement Valls*, named for Prime Minister Manuel Valls, who had assumed that position on March 31. The Scottish independence referendum, in which 55 percent of voters chose to remain within the United Kingdom, would take place a few weeks later, on September 18, 2014.

† Bernard Ollivier, *Aventures en Loire*, Phébus, 2009.

clouds. Our relationship is like our journey: determined, advancing at a steady, walking pace. If happiness is to be celebrated, then let us do so every day, for with Bénédicte, I feel immersed in the fullness of life. From the moment we met, we've laid bare our souls, without pretense, without one party attempting to impose itself on the other. This sweet and talented woman surprises me daily. I love her face, furrowed at a young age by laugh lines; her agile and hardworking hands; the energy she devotes to everything she does. Her place is near me, and mine, naturally, is near her. And, in this beautiful harmony, we always walk at the same pace.

In Travnik, we pick up a pair of pullovers, for we're going to have to camp in an ultra-lightweight tent bought for a hike in Italy's Po Valley last August. And we can't switch out our gear along the way. The humidity is oppressive. We hear that in northern Bosnia there are catastrophic floods, washed-out roads, and landslides. We worry about the weather as we get back underway, but the real difficulty will once again be the hellish traffic on the road to Sarajevo, as well as on the road to Zenica, the nation's largest industrial city. The pavement is narrow. We have to keep a close watch both ahead and behind, and when two trucks cross paths, we have no choice but to stop and step aside, for there's no more space for a pedestrian. We plan to cover fifteen and a half miles today. Will Bénédicte's knee hold up? At twelve and a half miles, the pain returns. But yes, it will hold up.

People told us that we'd find a place to stay in the large market town of Busovača. And what a place it is! The TISA is one of those delusions of grandeur communist regimes were so fond of, and of which, in Central Asia, I found many specimens. Local tyrants made sure that their region's hotels were built in proportion to their own, somewhat oversized, egos. This one boasts seventy-five guest rooms and a dining room large enough to seat six hundred and fifty . . . yet we're the only guests. They figure that, for such small fry as us, it isn't worth firing up the enormous kitchens. So we head downtown, where a bowl of soup at a restaurant perks us up. On our way back to the TISA, I feel a sudden severe pain in one of my ears. A pharmacist who was about to close shop and who speaks excellent English gives me some drops, antibiotics, and pain killers. Should I be alarmed? While talking about the patient-doctor relationship, the fellow utters a funny little maxim: "Listen only to yourself and your horse." In our bathroom at the hotel, probably on account of the floods, black water spews from the faucets, so we can't wash up.

Our maps put Sarajevo at a distance of 60 kilometers (37 miles). Nothing could be less certain, though, for a road sign tells us it's 93 kilometers (58 miles) away. Which should we believe? Just like every other day, the road is lined with graves, each one bearing a date. Here are some from the last world war, these over here are from the 1990s ethnic war, and now these over here are road fatalities. Each deadly accident has given rise to a more or less permanent memorial: a stone slab engraved with one or perhaps several names, artificial flowers, small monuments. There is nothing racist about the road: we find approximately as many Muslim names as Christian names.

We've been underway to Kiseljak for a good hour when, from a field overlooking the road, a brief invitation reaches our ears: "*Kava?*" A coffee? Of course! We never turn down coffee. The fellow's tall and about fifty years old; he has a wide, smiling face and a few tufts of sparse blond hair. A pair of eyeglasses hang down by a neck cord in front of his red sweater. Behind him is a metal shop, the name of which, METALEX, appears on the facade. In the court-yard, two young men are making something out of scrap metal. The man introduces himself: his name is Husmer. He suggests we park Ulysses, then leads us out in front of his workshop where, helped by one of his employees, he places a table and several chairs out in the sun. A curious armchair made of foam and lashed together with thick tape turns out to be quite comfortable. Our host treats us with warm and joyful consideration, thrilled to entertain these curious characters from so far away. Would Bénédicte like a cup of coffee, too? No, tea. Husmer has that, too. He asks us questions in German. When we tell him that our destination is Istanbul, he raises his arms to the sky and roars with laughter. His four employees join in the party too, interrupting their work to sip coffee with us. And the taste of that brew—though nothing special—is beyond compare. It's rich with the aroma of our encounter. Unfortunately, each of us has a rather limited knowledge of German; it then dawns on me to suggest a more concrete form of communion: that of fixing things. I show Husmer the threaded rod, which one of Ulysses's wheels attaches to. It's too long and is slightly bent from having smacked too many obstacles. It could use shortening. No one needs to translate. The five mechanics observing the rod have understood everything perfectly well. Husmer and his team leap into action. One of the men uncoils an electrical cord, another fetches a grinder, and the others offer their thoughts while going over our strange cart with a fine-tooth comb. A few minutes later, the rod is cut and filed down. Of course, when I offer him money, Husmer bursts out laughing. We snap a souvenir photo, shake the men's hard-working, grease-seasoned hands, then head back out onto the road, while the men return to their work. The shop's atmosphere positively oozes the joy of teamwork, and Husmer is transmitting this to his young employees, the oldest of whom is about thirty. And they all seem very happy to learn a trade here, in his company.

A smile like Husmer's could easily brighten our entire day, even as heavy clouds continue to crash into the hillsides. But another beautiful encounter awaits us in the little village of Brestovsko. Josefina returns our *dobar dan*, then stops us, intrigued by our cart. Perhaps sixty, she has a massive, busty frame and a girlish grin. Where are we from? She lights up at the word "France," but she wants to know more: how old is Bénédicte, how old am I, are we married, do we have children, and so on and so forth. When she finds out that we were born twenty-eight years apart, her reply is accompanied by a gesture that I can confidently translate as "You little devil!" while her eyes twinkle with laughter. She shoves us into the coffeehouse next door. Our conversation starts right back up with a little French, a little English, a smattering of German, and the rest in Bosnian. Josefina is sixty-one and has three children. They're all diabetic, like her deceased husband. A retiree, her income is about two hundred and forty dollars a month. But she insists on paying for our cups of coffee and wants to buy us all kinds of food and gifts, which we turn down with our deepest apologies. Josefina doesn't hold it against us and gives Bénédicte a big hug. In my notebook, she carefully inscribes her name, address, and phone numbers, all in caps. Muslim Husmer and Christian Josefina, but the very same openness to others.

Muslim villages alternate with Christian villages yet again. In one group, the mosque is empty; in the other, grass grows in front of the church's door. Here, that abominable practice of ethnic cleansing operated with scalpel-like precision. In the Muslim villages, none of the women are wearing hijabs or even simple scarves, apart from a few grandmothers. Scores of shops are devoted to gambling, the opium of the people. The men really get into it. Their eyes glued to TV screens, they fill out slips soon tossed to the floor. In Kiseljak, a young man, staring at his computer and frantically agitated, tells us that he's working on gaming software for a company in the Democratic Republic of the Congo. The algorithms he writes ensure that the machine never loses. Between these programs and the fellow himself, we can't help but wonder which is crazier, given the way his overexcited speech patterns make him impossible to understand.

As we're closing in on Sarajevo, a man raises his arm in a friendly gesture. His vest's other sleeve is empty. Farther along, with the rain picking up, an arm wielding a windshield wiper emerges from a car window and furiously goes to work so that the blinded driver doesn't wind up in the ditch. Welcome to a land of deep wounds and incredible resourcefulness, into that mythical city where culture could not prevent the hatred.

XII

SARAJEVO ROSES

On the sixth of September, we enter Sarajevo, not without a touch of pride at having overcome our journey's trials and kept our pledge to set foot here together, hand in hand. Just hearing the name of some cities can trigger the emotions. Sarajevo is one of these, just like, for me, Samarkand, and the name of the town I grew up in. Sarajevo: city of history, of memory, and of culture. Sarajevo: where, in 1914, one weapon's firing pin set all of Europe ablaze. Sarajevo: city of the 1984 Olympics. And, finally, the martyred city of Sarajevo: which, not even twenty years ago, suffered a dreadful siege.*

Setting out from Kiseljak, we reach the outskirts of the Bosnian capital on a kind of six-lane highway with traffic of Dantean proportions. Clearly, no one ever dreamed that hiking boots would one day venture out among so many tires. There's no shoulder, only what was probably intended to be a sidewalk with room for just one of our cart's wheels. Fearing that it will tip over onto the roadway, where cars would immediately smash it to pieces, one of us pulls Ulysses while the other makes sure he stays upright, but that exposes us even more to traffic. A heavy rain lashes us and makes the roadway slipperier than usual. The cars don't immediately see us, so they steer clear at the last moment. Each is a ticking time bomb. We're not about to get our first glimpse of Sarajevo and then die. We redouble

---

* TN: At three years and ten months, the Siege of Sarajevo was the longest in the history of modern warfare (April 5, 1992–February 29, 1996).

our vigilance. We're finally saved by a waiter out front of a restaurant, who points us to a less-congested side road.

We pass near the "Tunnel of Hope." It was through this half-mile-long underground passageway, dug beneath the airport over a period of four months, that the besieged population was able to bring in food and, thanks to a telephone cable, remain in touch with the outside world for the entire 1,394 days of the siege. Prior to its construction, snipers picked off the fathers and brothers who tried crossing the airfield out in the open, hoping to find food for their families.

Despite the best intentions of those you meet, in Bosnia, it's very hard to get your bearings. People are extremely courteous, and everyone stops to help. But since they don't like to say "no"—or worse, "I have no idea"—they simply point a hand in a particular direction and proclaim that it's "over there, farther on." We're soaked to the bone, frozen stiff, and desperate to find the youth hostel where, cautious this time, we reserved ahead. A young woman on her way back home gives us shelter from the storm beneath her building's front awning. She takes the time to look up our hostel on her cell. Not finding it, she dials her husband who locates the information on his computer. On my notepad, she sketches detailed directions for the hostel. Sadly, when we get there, they have no record of our reservation. A young woman confesses that she forgot to jot it down, and now they're full up. Our legs cry uncle at this stroke of bad luck and so, fed up, we hail a taxi. The driver, a forty-five-year-old Bosniak war veteran, shares with us his bitterness at having fought "for nothing." He works twelve hours a day for a paltry paycheck. Completely disillusioned, he's come to detest Sarajevo, a city he once loved and was ready to die for "back when it was Yugoslavian and socialist. Not communist, mind you."

Downtown, the walls speak, and nationalism—that poison, which again led to the spilling of blood here twenty years ago—is on display all about. A beekeeper has gone as far as to conscript his bees: he painted his hives the colors of his flag, then lined them up on a hillside. Graffiti gets in on the act as well. But there are expressions of

"NEVER AGAIN," too. We come to a dead stop in front of a wall on which huge letters spell out: "NEVER FORGET SREBRENICA!"

Barely into our hotel room, we crash and sleep for ten hours straight. A little detail we notice with surprised amusement suggests that respect for others is of utmost importance here: the door to the communal toilet can't be locked from the inside. It's either open and one can go in, or it's closed and the toilet's in use. We have to be careful not to close the door out of habit upon leaving, as that could cause quite a commotion!

Eager to dive right into the city's history, we discover that, hemmed in by high hills under Serbian control, Sarajevo found itself in a trap. We begin our tour at Parkuša Park.* During the siege, every inch of its soil was used, either for growing vegetables or for burying the dead. Countless Muslim gravestones are scattered about. In fact, they're nothing more than sculpted granite posts, with tops often shaped like turbans. Here, with so many people milling about, life once again rubs shoulders with death. At the edge of the park, a monument has been erected to the ten thousand civilians who died during the siege. Farther on, the names of the 1,600 children killed over three years are engraved on revolving vertical scrolls: that amounts to just over one child per day. Here, too, house facades are riddled with bullet holes, most now filled in. After the conflict, residents poured red resin into them—those "Sarajevo roses"—or transformed them into stars. We walk down "Sniper Alley," a wide boulevard that Serbian sharpshooters had in their crosshairs. To traverse it, Sarajevans grabbed their bags or their kid and ran as fast as they could. Death came discreetly. Far from the gunmen, each victim fell in silence, for the sound of the detonation arrived long after the bullet. I shudder to think that a person nearby must have heard nothing but the soft sound of the projectile ripping through flesh and snapping bones.

---

* TN: Known today as Veliki (meaning "larger") Park.

The Historical Museum of Bosnia and Herzegovina is poorly designed, poorly lit, and poorly laid out, but absolutely gripping. Take, for example, this photograph of a huge peace demonstration which, in defiance of the fever pitch of violent nationalisms that preceded the fighting, challenged politicians to preserve peace. Black-and-white photos; fascinating faces, full of determination and courage. I'm moved to tears by a particular shot of a solemn, pensive little girl. Pinned to her shoulder is a badge bearing a peace slogan. Was she one of the 1,600 children killed in Sarajevo, or one of the thousands of others the ogre devoured elsewhere? Bénédicte and I occasionally pore over the photographs of the delighted faces of children we took during our trek across Syria and get all choked up. What became of them in that hellhole? Were they ripped to pieces by shellfire or, on the road to exile, are they walking towards Europe, just as it's starting to slam shut its doors? War kills indiscriminately.

One exhibit conveys the violence of those hate-filled, desperate days. Its creator photographed the city's main buildings both during and after the conflict, from the same angle each time. They reveal thousands of bullet holes, building exteriors blackened by fire, half-collapsed structures. The effect is striking. But stones weren't the only thing the war shattered, as evidenced by the photos of this baby with one leg blown off, and of a teen boy with two severed hands—they seem to glare reproachfully at the entire world. We did nothing for these people, or what we did was too little, or too late. Look at the calm, admirable courage of this woman hanging laundry out on her apartment's balcony, bent out of shape by a shell that tore off its glass door as well. And the courage of the reporters on this other photo who, each day of the siege, published an edition of *Oslobodenje*, their newspaper, and to hell with the snipers, the paper shortage, the power blackouts. They sometimes typed their stories on loose leaf, then tacked them to trees that had somehow escaped being felled for firewood. People had to hold strong and figure out how to eat, dress, and go on living in spite of it all. Like this inventor who, using parts from a wrecked car, constructed a small waterwheel on the river. Day in and day out, it generated electricity to charge up a battery. Or these rifles manufactured from lengths of pipe, with butts carved using pocketknives. The assassins shooting at civilians from high overhead did not win this war. Quite the contrary: they turned this martyred city into a shining example admired throughout the world. Each stone of Sarajevo is part of an immense monument to human resistance and courage.

This strength of will is nothing new. In a humble restaurant near the Miljacka River, we learn about one of its former owners. In the nineteenth century, the fellow was already an old man when the occupying Austro-Hungarian forces decided to confiscate his property to build a palace on it worthy of their mightiness. The simple but determined old man fought back with such energy that the Empire had to admit defeat and erect that monument to its own glory somewhere else.

Ruined iconostases, burned-down mosques and churches: the hatred was not directed only at people. Today, at the heart of the city, the Muslim mosque, the Protestant church, the Catholic cathedral, and the Jewish temple are shoulder to shoulder—although the door of the latter building is reinforced with steel and secured with four pad-locks. Places of worship, places of violence.

In one of the galleries, there's an exhibition on the city of Srebrenica. This cold-hearted genocide is presented in a staggering way. Written documents and videos depict, in gruesome detail, how eight thousand men and adolescents were sorted, herded, executed, then dumped into mass graves, where bulldozers crushed their bodies so that they would be beyond recognition. Visitors hear testimony from women who were raped, and from others whose husbands and sons were led away and killed. They will never know where, nor when, their loved ones died. And this soldier over here, machine gun in hand, who, leading a man to his execution, asks, "Are you scared?"

then fires a volley of bullets into his back. And Ratko Mladić, the butchers' leader, who gave the UN representative his word that his hostages would not be executed if NATO stopped bombing his troops' positions. He got what he wanted, then gave the order for the massacre to begin.*

Though this pause in Sarajevo gives our bodies a chance to relax, our spirits, on the other hand, cannot, given how deeply moved we are by these visions of horror, this massacre of the innocents in full view of UN peacekeepers, who turned out to be powerless to protect them. "I can no longer look at a Serbian man over forty without wondering whether he was involved," Bénédicte tells me, as we exit the exhibition.

The next leg of our journey stretches across a portion of the Republika Srpska.† Each time we reach a border, we snap a souvenir selfie in front of the new country's sign. For this one, my companion puts on a frown. It's true that the country might not have substantively changed. Radovan Karadžić, wanted for war crimes and genocide and, in particular, for the siege of Sarajevo and the Srebrenica Massacre, managed to "hide" out in the open for thirteen years, simply by keeping to his hometown. Once peacetime returned, he altered his appearance, changed his name, gave up his career as a psychiatrist, and went into . . . natural medicine. Although it wasn't as if he had been protected by all one-and-a-half million citizens of the Republika Srpska, without the support of some of them, he could have never remained at large for so long.

---

* TN: A Bosnian Serb, Ratko Mladić, born 1942, was head of the Army of Republika Srpska during the Bosnian War, from 1992 to 1995. For his role in the massacres, he became known as "The Butcher of Bosnia." In 2017, he was found guilty of war crimes, crimes against humanity, and genocide, and was sentenced to life in prison. His final appeal was rejected in June 2021.
† TN: The Republika Srpska (or Serbian Republic of Bosnia) comprises the zones of Bosnia and Herzegovina populated primarily by Serbs.

Tomorrow, we'll be on his turf, in his hometown of Pale. He, though, is behind bars at the International Court of Justice in The Hague, waiting to be judged on eleven counts. The prosecution seeks a life sentence.*

---

* TN: A guilty verdict was later rendered on March 24, 2016. Karadžić was sentenced to forty years in prison. His appeal was rejected on March 20, 2019, and his sentence increased to life.

XIII

TUNNELS

*The Republika Srpska (*Република Српска*). Population: 1.4 million. Not recognized as an independent state. Non-member of the European Union. Outside the Eurozone. Capital cities: Banja Luka and Sarajevo.*

The region known as Bosnia and Herzegovina looks very much like it was created by a mad politician with a fondness for jigsaw puzzles. The Republika Srpska consists, in fact, of two zones. To Sarajevo's north is the former Bosanska Krajina region and its de facto capital city, Banja Luka. East of Sarajevo lies another entity, with Banja Luka as its capital as well, in addition to the Istočno Sarajevo District (East Sarajevo), its de jure capital. In practice, most of the Republika Srpska's official institutions are in Banja Luka. Currently, the polity is recognized on the world stage as a de facto state within Bosnia and Herzegovina only. And so, still trying to wrap our minds around this complicated situation, we set foot into a country that isn't really a country. Our first stop will be Pale. It's a walk in the park: an expected eleven miles after a two-day rest—we won't be wearing ourselves out. Still, breaking away from the charms of Sarajevo is, in and of itself, a huge mental challenge, but a physical one, too: we have to ascend to an 850-meter-high (2,800-foot) mountain pass beneath a broiling sun. But the hardest part of the journey will be the tunnels. Bénédicte's skittish at the thought of plunging in. So, in setting out, we avoid the most direct route, which involves a long underground tunnel at the city's edge: too bad if it means doing a detour. Our walk begins with "Ambassadors Alley." There's a little marble plaque for each diplomat who performed a tour of duty in Sarajevo, each bearing the diplomat's name and country. When we finally reach the main road, the tunnel is behind us. My companion can breathe again, but not for long. Three miles farther, a rocky ridge prevents anyone from crossing it except through a tunnel, and, to make matters worse, we have no idea how long it might be. It's indicated only . . . at the other end. To make matters worse, it's a cramped space, and if two cars cross paths, there won't be any room for Ulysses. We take out our headlamps to make up for the few lightbulbs on the walls, which are covered in dust and soot from all the gas and diesel fumes: a coating that blocks light. The sidewalk is just the right height for Ulysses to get one wheel up but is too narrow for both. Barely sixty feet in, a crater in the roadway throws our buggy off balance; he performs a somersault and winds up wheels in the air, smack dab in the middle of the roadway. We grab him lickety-split and drag him out of the way of the cars roaring in our direction. That was close! I tow Ulysses from the front while Bénédicte, with one hand on him, readies to right him should we come to another chuckhole, but that puts her a little farther out into the road. After having gone about a thousand feet, shaking in our boots each time truck meets car, we suddenly find ourselves in total darkness. Behind us, far off in the distance, is the tunnel's entrance—a tiny point of light. Ahead, it's black as night, for there are no more lightbulbs. Our dim headlamps let us see only our feet. The cars coming head-on blind us, then leave us in the shadows. Bénédicte pulls some reflective armbands from her bag, which she had the foresight to purchase for walking at night. We cinch them around our arms and ankles. We feel our way forward, not knowing whether we have to keep going straight or if the tunnel starts to turn. Bénédicte, taut as a bowstring, galvanized by the danger, pushes Ulysses along with such force that she could easily throw me off balance and make me fall. I shout back at her to stop, but, deaf from the noise of all the engines echoing off the walls, she can't hear a thing. Finally, after a two- or three-hundred-yard-long nightmare, a final bend to the left lets us glimpse a faint light. It's the other entrance. I let go of Ulysses and take my wife in my arms. Half laughing with relief, releasing her pent-up fear, she bombards me with words, trying to tell me, in total disorder, all that she's been wanting to say, but couldn't, due to the darkness and the noise. We're safely through . . . this time, anyhow.

We soon come to two more tunnels with a particular feature: the sidewalk, just as narrow as in the first, consists of cement slabs, some of which are broken. Traveling on it would be to risk falling and getting hurt. We have no choice but to roll along the roadway itself. Thankfully, that second tunnel isn't very long. In the third, which I estimate to be about five hundred feet long in a straight line, I make the most of a break in the traffic, take a deep breath, then start running, throwing all caution to the wind. Bénédicte, caught off-guard for a split second, first hesitates, then follows my lead, laughing and yelling all the way: "You're nuts! You're a madman, and I love you!" My impulsive behavior turns out to be a stressbuster. From now on, we know we can handle tunnels. The Stabulcic Tunnel, at over 900 meters (3,000 feet) above sea level, is 945 meters long. By some extraordinary stroke of luck, we meet only four cars in it.

Pale is but a small market town, yet it was frequently in the news when Karadžić made it the Bosnian Serbs' "capital." Since his arrest, the city has fallen back into the drab obscurity it knew before the carnage.

We turn onto a little road that leads us through villages. The few inhabitants we meet observe us from a distance. That makes it hard for us to ask people which way we should go. As we're closing in on Podgrab, a man comes up to us and invites us for a beer. Radislav Simovic is very approachable. He questions us, expresses surprise, then leads us to his house which, last spring, was flooded by a small nearby river that snowmelt had turned into a torrent of mud. He has us sit down on plastic chairs and a handsome stool carved with a billhook and buffed by generations of trousers. "I'm Orthodox," he tells us, as if that mattered. When I ask him whether there are any

Muslims in his village, he makes a "good riddance" gesture, then points to another village, higher up in the hills. Here, he says, all the "Turks" are gone. It's a term Serbs often use to refer to Muslims. He utters something that official "ethnic cleansing" propaganda must have repeated over and over for months and years: "The Turks came here four hundred years ago, weapons in hand." Which, of course, justifies eliminating their children fifteen generations later in the same way . . . His face, which had gone stern, softens up again as he adds, as if to reassure us: "You'll find some farther along." This friendly, hospitable man: did he join in the fighting, too? In 1992, he would have been in his early forties, no doubt in his prime. Rather than sidestep the issue, he confesses that he once subscribed to the "Greater Serbia" ideology, which was the driving force behind ethnic cleansing. "There were a lot of deaths here between 1992 and 1995, but now, we need peace, with Europe." Bénédicte snaps a photo of me next to him. He's ten inches taller than me and likely weighs twice as much. We're like Laurel and Hardy. He's retired and hardly ever travels. His wife, who's a teacher, and one of his sons both work in Sarajevo where, he grumbles, there are no longer all that many Serbs or Croats. His second son lives in New York City. Leaving Radislav's house, we are more aware of how, in people's minds, suspicions, long-simmering animosities and desires for revenge still linger. So long as those responsible have not been brought to justice, such feelings will remain tucked away, ready to spring back to life. The verdicts that judges in The Hague eventually arrive at will either bring lasting peace . . . or fan the flames of new fighting.

Hrenovica is a tiny town with no accommodations for travelers. We wander about and ask futile questions for an hour, then a car stops with two pretty women on board.

"Are you looking for a *sobe*?"

"Yes, how do you know?"

Their uncle, whom we had run into a short while earlier and who told us that he couldn't think of anywhere we could sleep, must have got to thinking that a good opportunity should never be wasted.

What the women have is better than a room: it's a house. Before we know it, we're sitting at a table outside, enjoying tea and nibbling on grilled corn in the company of Suleyman, the father, Nerma, the mother, and their daughters, Emina and Mersida. After the usual small talk, the two young ladies take us to a nearby house that belongs to another uncle of theirs, one who lives in Holland. They offer to let us spend the night there for the modest sum of twenty euros, which we gladly accept. And it's a pleasant evening, for Suleyman has harvested from his greenhouse fresh tomatoes and peppers, which we use to cook up a festive dinner.

Radislav tells us that there are two roads to Goražde: one through the valley, the other through the mountains. Like any good motorist would, he suggests we take the low-lying road, but we opt instead for the hills. In one village, a woman comes smiling our way with her hand outstretched: *"Dobro jutro!"* (Good morning!); she then utters a phrase containing the word *kava*. We reason that she's offering us a cup of coffee. "Yes, of course!" we tell her, delighted. To our great surprise, after a smile and a little farewell wave, she turns around and walks off. Confused, we eventually surmise that she must have asked us whether we had *already* had coffee. Faced with our "yes," she didn't insist.

In a hamlet, a woman steps out of a house, greets us, exchanges a few words with us, promising: "I'll put you up on your way back!" then vanishes. Does she think we're making a round trip?

It's already half past noon by the time we crest the mountain pass at 1,200 meters (4,000 feet). The view's fabulous, but big black clouds are rolling in, and my barometer's little needle has started going crazy. We're still nine miles from Goražde. We hurriedly make our way back down from the pass, stopping along the road to lunch on a can of sardines, a small hunk of bread, and a raw green pepper. But we're still hungry. A motorist pulls up and asks whether there's a hotel-restaurant—we're looking for one too—and drives off. Fifteen minutes later, he's back, having found a restaurant further down in the valley, but to get there, we'd have to go way off course. Our stomachs opt for the extra distance. The hotel turns out to be a small winter-sports resort named Bijele Vode (blue water). A small ski-tow and a grooming machine, fast asleep, will spring back to life as soon as the first snow falls which, at this altitude and season, might be any day now.

Here are some interesting facts about the village of Bijele Vode: in 1971, it was inhabited by 117 Serbs and one Croat. The 2013 census, though, found zero inhabitants. Every last one left between 1991 and 1996. Today, only the hotel and a mineral water bottling facility remain. A few houses sit empty but are in good condition. Perhaps their former owners come back from time to time, or maybe they're used by ski resort employees. A dozen tiny chalets, all identical, lie scattered about a specially maintained area. No sooner do we sit down to eat than the storm lashes out over the valley. The pouring rain doesn't let up until later that evening.

The other guests are hunters who have assembled here for a battue tomorrow. Some came all the way from Slovenia, hoping to bag a few "trophy" animals. The owner warns us that there's a *privât* concert this evening, but that if we dine, we won't have to pay admission for the music. The band consists of a charming keyboard player whose face exudes infinite sadness, a smiling accordionist, and a singer who carries his voice with as much self-assurance as he carries his belly out in front of him. In terms of sound, we're spoiled. For seven hours, the band thunders away with amplifiers cranked to the max; at the same time, a large television set retransmits a lively parliamentary debate, and the hunters boast loudly of their many exploits. Large jugs of water are set out on each table, along with other, slightly smaller ones, filled to the brim with *jabuka*, a strong alcohol that everyone insists we try. When I ask how the beverage is made, an old man, as thin as a rail, but surely a crack shot when he's sober, holds up an apple. So, it's an alcohol that everyone from Normandy knows well: Calvados.* Still, other than to wet my lips, I turn it down. When

---

* TN: An apple brandy made in Ollivier's home region of Normandy.

you're on a long-distance walk, alcohol becomes impossible to force down. I will, from time to time, quaff a glass of wine, but never the strong stuff, which I don't much like anyway.

The small carafes go empty faster than the large ones: the amount of alcohol consumed is staggering. Muhamad invites us to sit at his table and buys us a round of drinks. He explains that, as far as alcohol is concerned, Bosniak Muslims do not observe every single precept in the Qur'an. The conversations' volume rises as the level of *jabuka* in the carafes drops. The accordion snores away, and the singer, who's in fact quite a virtuoso, wanders from table to table. Whenever a man—Bénédicte being the only woman—wishes to show his appreciation, he slips a banknote into one of the accordion's bellows, which, before long, is abristle with bills. When they become too many, the artist nimbly snatches them all up. The band indiscriminately takes requests for music from every Balkan country, that is to say, tunes from Macedonia, Serbia, Croatia, and Bosnia. After struggling to keep other guests from refilling our glasses, we bid the howling assembly a good night. Muhamad suggests we call him the next morning when we reach Goražde, where he lives.

To get to Goražde, we have to drag Ulysses over a dirt path to the top of a mountain pass at 1,200 meters (4,000 feet), but the climb is well worth it. To our left, a summit at 1,600 meters; to our right, the view extends out to infinity. What an incredibly beautiful country! I will marvel, all throughout our journey across the Balkans, at how rich the forests are. Every species of tree is here, beech being the most prevalent. If it were up to me, I'd rather be buried in a forest than in a cemetery, where, for just a few days each year, the only live plants are chrysanthemums. I feel communion with every trunk, every branch, every leaf. Trees stir my emotions in all seasons. In the spring, when forests pump billions of gallons of sap to the skies; in the summer, when chlorophyll repaints the landscape in shaded tones of green; in the fall, when forests burst into flames of red, yellow, and toasty gold; and in the winter, when bare trees, sometimes sprinkled with snow, fortify their roots while they patiently await springtime's grand thaw.

They embody—steadfastly, stubbornly—the miraculous routine of life. And here, they quiet the ghosts of the dead roaming around us. During our two-hour descent, on average, we see one roadside-fatality memorial per kilometer. The majority of photos depict young people.

Rounding a bend, the tragedy that Goražde endured appears before us. On some kind of balcony overlooking the city, a tank and two heavy machine guns sit rusting away, their barrels aimed at the dwellings just below, on either side of the Drina River. Like Sarajevo, Goražde was surrounded and besieged. Before the war, its population was one-third Bosno-Serb and two-thirds Bosniak (Muslim). No sooner had the hostilities begun, than Muslims living in the outlying areas abandoned their homes to looters and took refuge inside the city. Orthodox Christians fled. The Serbian Army and its militias positioned themselves overhead and the shelling began. A detachment of UN peacekeepers was sent in to protect the city's inhabitants, but it pulled out when the pressure grew too great. An incomprehensible decision. How could soldiers abandon unarmed civilians? From that moment on, tank and mortar fire rained down nonstop. The trapped population, holed up in shelters, went through hell. In a few weeks' time, nearly seven hundred residents had been killed and two thousand injured. Like Sarajevo, Mostar, and Srebrenica, Goražde became a city of martyrs. But the people of the "Goražde Enclave" were abandoned not only by the UN, but by the international press as well, which, faced with an onslaught of horror stories, turned its focus mostly to Sarajevo and Srebrenica. Perhaps it was out of belated remorse that, when the Dayton Agreement was drawn up, it was decided that Goražde's Muslim population could remain in the city, even though it would be an enclave within the Republika Srpska. A "land corridor" allows inhabitants to travel freely to the Federation of Bosnia and Herzegovina, and to Sarajevo. It's very narrow at one end and could, at any moment, be closed by a few tanks or a handful of soldiers, and, in several hours, the city would be surrounded yet again.

In town, by chance, we run into our friend Muhamad seated outside a restaurant with a female acquaintance, sipping mineral water to recover from all the *jabuka* he drank last night. The pair tells us what the city was like during the siege. Each building tries to hide its wounds. Spackle masks bullet holes in facades, but the job was never completed, so the buildings look as if they were decorated by impressionist—or perhaps pointillist—painters.

From the restaurant terrasse, we can see Izetbegović Bridge, named for the Bosniak president who proclaimed the country's independence. A footbridge, it's a place where people living downtown like to meet up. People both young and old stride along it at dinner time. Beneath it, hanging by cables from the deck, is a kind of gangway, over which the wounded were carried to the hospital across the river. That's because anyone venturing out onto the bridge itself would have met certain death, riddled with bullets raining down from the sky. An underground tunnel in Sarajevo, a secret gangway in Goražde . . . To survive, you had to be willing to give up the sky, which was the domain of the gods . . . and of the assassins.

From the start of the conflict, people crammed into the few houses that hadn't been destroyed; they ate when they could find food; they went into survival mode. Those who could fled the mayhem, like Muhamad. He and his family left the city soon after the fighting began and, when the war finally caught up with him, he went into exile in Denmark, in Jutland. He still lives there with his family and is now a Danish citizen; he comes back to the land of his birth only for vacation, hoping to soak up the sun before the Nordic winter sets in. In Bosnia, nearly one million citizens out of five are expats and will never return home.*

---

* TN: Bosnia and Herzegovina's 2022 population was an estimated 3.2 million, down from 3.5 in 2020, and 4.4 in 1991. In 2020, the World Bank reported that nearly half of all Bosnians were living outside Bosnia and that emigration was still at a high level (*Bosnia and Herzegovina: Systematic Diagnostic Country Update.* Washington, DC: The World Bank, 18–19).

Muhamad, stoic despite his hangover, is a valuable guide in our quest for a set of tires to replace Ulysses's current ones, which have rolled all the way from France. They're completely spent, right down to the casing. After seven or eight shops, we're forced to face the facts: we'll never find tires that fit. The Russian-made rims were taken from a kid's bike in Uzbekistan. Since I can't find tires, I buy new wheels. What difference does it make if they're not exactly the same size? My knack for fixing things comes from having grown up poor: we had no toys, let alone a bike, other than those we cobbled together ourselves with parts found here and there, without worrying what the end result looked like. The inner tubes of the first bike I built were such a palimpsest of rubber patches that there was never a day I didn't have to do a repair job. Which, by force of habit, I became quite good at.

With Ulysses now proudly perched atop his new wheels, we head out of the city by way of the bridge over the Drina, where a heart-rending monument stops us in our tracks. It commemorates the hundred and twenty children killed during the siege.* In the foreground, a cut-out steel plaque represents the profiles of three children holding hands. Behind them, the names of all the children are engraved on an immense black slab. Next to each name are two dates, a birth date and a death date. The oldest child was twelve. Some died in their first month of life. For others, only a birth date is given. Were they killed in their mother's womb, or on the day they were born?

The road out of the city is tough: it climbs from 350 to 800 meters (1,150 to 2,600 feet) over a short distance. One odd house facade bears the design of a large circle of bricks. The owner, an old woman, confirms my suspicions: a shell crashed into her home. They quickly plugged the hole back up with available materials. Farther on, a large thirteen-by-twenty-foot billboard, like those used for expensive

---

* TN: The exact number of children killed in Goražde is unknown, but was probably considerably higher than this figure.

advertisements back home, displays a regional map with large red areas on it. Those are the minefields. It will be years before they can be reopened to locals. Traveling cross-country is still completely out of the question.

Around a bend, the Le Paris restaurant displays its name alongside a roughly sketched Eiffel Tower. The owner's father lives in France's capital city. Second-rate food and nasty bathrooms: the place doesn't do much for Paris's image. With rain coming down, we get back on the road to Metaljka, a city at the Montenegrin border. In Miljeno, a tiny village, it starts pouring so heavily that we decide to duck into a woodshed for cover. A woman dashes out of the house next door who at first gives us a surprised look, then yells something that, by the tone of her voice, clearly means: "What are you doing on my property?!" She's immediately joined by a young man who can speak a few words of broken English and we explain what we're up to. Their tone changes just as a ray of summer sunshine replaces the downpour.

"Come on in for some coffee!"

The young man, who's seventeen, introduces himself: he's a Christian, a Serbian. Only then does he tell us his first name: Aleksandar. Milicia, his mother, or more likely his grandmother, pesters him to translate the questions running through her head. She serves us each a glass of fruit juice, then a cup of coffee, which she calls "Bosniak" rather than "Turkish." When we ask her if any Muslims still reside in the community, she makes the orthodox sign of the cross and, gesturing with her two hands, says: "With a broom, they've been swept away. Good riddance!" To which she adds: "You won't run into any from here all the way to the border," as if to reassure us.

As we're closing in on Čajaniče, a hamlet perched at eight hundred meters (2,600 feet), a young girl with a deadpan face, about ten years old, makes the sign of the cross to let us know that, if we're Muslim, we might as well keep right on going. Still unsure, she asks us what our religion is. We pretend not to understand. For certain Bosnian Serbs, you identify yourself first as Orthodox, then as Serbian, then finally, if those first two criteria are met, you are worthy of having a name.

Someone told us there was a hotel here, but it's closed. We ask passers-by if we might find a *sobe* somewhere else. A middle-aged woman offers us her second-floor bedroom. The twenty euros we hand her make her blush with delight. The next morning, I discover that she spent the night in her day clothes on the couch downstairs. Try as we might, we can't seem to make her understand who we are and what we're doing. As we're heading out, two police officers show up and look like they're going to question her. Are they going to issue her a ticket, or do they want their share of the twenty euros? She slams the door behind us as we wander off.

The Orthodox church built at the village's highest point is the center of community social life. A young woman weeps in front of the iconostasis, transfixed before an icon of the Virgin with Child. Very unfamiliar with the Orthodox Church, we watch a man exit the shrine: he walks backwards toward the door, makes the sign of the cross (right shoulder, left shoulder), kisses the crucifix on the left door, makes the sign of the cross yet again, kisses the crucifix on the right door, then finally turns around and heads home. The mosque, located a short distance away, has been repaired after having suffered damage during the hostilities. It seems to be empty, but a pair of flip-flops makes us think that someone must be inside and locked the door. During our stay, the minaret's loudspeakers never once broadcast the call to prayer.

The road to Pljevlja climbs abruptly inside a narrow canyon, and we walk between two fir-tree walls. The customs agent, a woman with a contagious laugh sitting with her colleagues inside one of those prefab worksite shacks, glances at Bénédicte's passport and says, with a rolled "r": *"Bonjourrrr, Madame! Comment allez-vous?"* That's all she remembers from her childhood French courses. But it's a source of great pride.

Farewell, battered and bruised Bosnia! We leave you with the customs officer's laughter still ringing in our ears. We now set foot into one of the smallest of the Balkan nations.[*]

---

[*] TN: The smallest is Kosovo (4,203 mi²), just after Montenegro (5,333 mi²).

* * *

Goražde—September 12

We spend the first part of our lives looking for something to hold onto, and the second, letting go.

The Bosnians, for their part, do not worry about this dilemma.

Slowness and patience are of the essence here.

People wait around a lot, especially in cafes—the men, that is, of course—who sip their kava *or local* pivo* *in silence, admirably taking their time. Elbows on the bar counter, lost in thought while staring out into the street (or at the back of someone else staring out into the street), they pass the day smoking like chimneys. A pack of smokes goes for half a euro here, and, on that topic, the women are the men's equals.*

People wait for buses at mysterious stops out in the middle of nowhere. Or for their brother-in-law to drive up in his classic Volkswagen mini-bus, cloaked in a nasty black cloud, a small blemish in the clear mountain sky.

People wait for the materials they need to finish the second floor of their house, or for the stucco to finish the home they rebuilt after the war with money from Europe, but which was only enough to erect a first floor. One house in four is in ruins, the other three are either abandoned, for sale, or unfinished. Depressing sights.

People wait for a real job, in addition to whatever they already do under the table; for a more reasonable pension; or for perhaps a pair of dentures. How many toothless smiles have returned our greetings, disfiguring the beautiful faces of women not yet fifty?

They're all waiting, in any case, for a better, more peaceful future.

The two days we spent in Sarajevo (finally, a beautiful and truly charming city!), and the one spent in Goražde, has given us a sense of

---

* TN: Beer.

just how horrible this atrocious war was, waged in part against civilians in order to eliminate, convert, or drive away the other.

Four years of siege for Sarajevo and Goražde. Several hundred thousand dead throughout the country, including eight thousand men and adolescents massacred in Srebrenica in full view of UN peacekeepers, who did nothing to stop it. Over two million displaced persons. Sarajevo's National Library was deliberately torched, sending a million volumes up in smoke, including 150,000 rare books and manuscripts. Ruins everywhere, even today, twenty years on.

How could you forget when you live in a building riddled with bullet holes?

When each day you walk past a map or a sign indicating the location of landmines?

How can you pardon the unpardonable?

A "war for nothing" is how Muhamad in Goražde summed it up. A war whose indelible marks constantly haunt us throughout our slow crossing of this incredibly beautiful country.

And yet, the people are staggeringly kind.

Even the cops smile as our little caravan passes by; it sure beats having them ask us for our papers or yelling at us for walking on the roadway!

Dogs don't bark at us either. Abandoned or feral, they wander by the hundreds at the edges of depressing landfills surrounded by pristine wilderness. Every now and then, a dog follows us, usually a puppy (irresistible!), incredibly happy to have found some company. But we have to chase it away, for the way it zigzags down the road puts us in danger. Two clowns and a cart suffice: cars don't need a fourth target as well.

The dead here exist among the living, or vice versa. Muslim graves are everywhere—between two buildings, along a city street, in a field—without fences or gravestones. They're elegant obelisks, often topped with carved turbans, which have seemingly sprung up out in the middle of a clearing, leaning this way or that. An Orthodox or Catholic cemetery is never very far, though most often just outside town: it takes more room to squeeze in sandstone slabs. Even the dead have their residential neighborhoods!

Contrary to all expectations, this proximity to death is soothing and pleasant. It makes life seem more precious, like our journey.

Otherwise, we're having a jolly old time! My companion—always in a good mood (except when we happen upon a real jerk, who risks finding himself on the receiving end of Bernard's ire!) and often singing—guides our buggy around curves with a masterful hand (a nudge to the right, a nudge to the left, depending on whether we can see around it), while I handle public relations, our third-rate Serbo-Bosno-Croat dictionary in hand, so that we find what we're looking for. It's no easy task. Especially since very few people speak English. We have somewhat better luck with German.

Our inability to speak their language is one heck of an obstacle, and I've sworn I'll never travel in countries where I can't communicate again. We'll see how that pans out.

Walking without signposts turns out to be a real chore, one that I enjoy learning day by day. We have to figure out which way to go, where to eat, where to sleep, where to fill up on water, and where we can relieve ourselves, especially me. And, for the first time ever, I find myself wishing I were one of the guys, especially in populated areas where we move from commercial zones to industrial zones with no hope whatsoever of ever finding that perfect little shrub. It's a full-time job tracking down abandoned worksites or transformers where you can duck out of sight to uncover your bum! For me, it's more out of respect for others (especially in Muslim countries) than out of modesty. Consequently, I'm not always as careful as I ought to be, especially since it's something I do at least twenty times a day—those four daily liters of water have to be eliminated somehow! One morning, thinking I was well-hidden behind a pile of sand, I looked up while pulling up my pants and saw five laughing fellows high atop the roof across the street.

The mind, which turns out to be very much in demand, struggles to set sail, except on long climbs to mountain passes, which take us from one *valley to another, when the road is deserted. At those times, I taste what Marie-Hélène Lafon describes so well, and what I, too, was seeking on this journey: "The slowness we need to pull ourselves back together."**

BF

---

* TN: Marie-Hélène Lafon, *Les Pays*, Paris: Éditions Buchet/Chastel, 2012.

XIV

MONTENEGRO

Montenegro (Crna Gora—meaning "black mountain"). Population: 620,000, and a large diaspora. Independence: 2006. Montenegro unilaterally adopted the euro as its standard currency. Capital city: Podgorica.

Customs checkpoints are ordinarily close to one another. But going from the jovial Bosniak customs officer to the border of Montenegro takes a three-hour climb. At a place known as Metaljka, two or three houses are huddled around the customs office. The officers ask us about our journey and tell us that Pljevlja is forty kilometers (twenty-five miles) away. Between here and there, would there by chance be a restaurant or hotel? No, nothing. A storm blows in and our morale takes a hit. The first drops begin to fall while we're eating the meager provisions we brought with us, only two hundred yards beyond the border crossing. A car, having just left the customs agents, rolls to a stop. A woman steps out and, without a word, brings us two apples and two snack cakes, then, still smiling and saying nothing, climbs back into the car, which drives off. Welcome to Montenegro.

The war, with all its scars, never crossed the border. The houses are beautiful; they're covered in colorful stuccoes and are well-maintained. Here, none have been abandoned. The Montenegrins we encounter are friendly and relaxed. Peace is a beautiful thing! The weather, though, not so much: heavy drops produce round, black splotches on the pavement. The idea of camping at 1,000 meters

(3,280 feet) in nasty weather is not our idea of fun. "Take the bus," a man suggests. We ask two workmen loading a truck whether they can tell us when it comes by.

"In four hours, but if it's to Pljevlja you want to go, there's no need to wait, we can take you there and even find you a room."

In no time at all, we've hoisted Ulysses up onto the truck's tarped bed where there's already a sofa and two armchairs on casters. The journey, though very short, is full of curves and we have a good laugh. Well-padded seat cushions soften the countless potholes. After a side trip to deliver the furniture, they drop us off just outside the city at the home of one of the driver's friends, who rents out rooms. And that's the very moment the storm decides to flood the countryside in an icy deluge. Phew! Thank you, guardian angel!

That evening, we have a candid heart-to-heart. In two days, we'll be in Serbia. Bénédicte, still reeling from what she saw and learned about Sarajevo, Srebrenica, and Goražde, wants nothing more to do with the Serbs or with Serbia, and is now balking at the idea of going there. Whereas for me, my background as a journalist makes me want to do just the opposite.

What should we do?

We'll figure that out later. Right now, let's go for a walk.

In Montenegro, a postage-stamp country, contemplation is apparently a full-time activity, given that there's a chair or recliner out in front of every house. Even when the dwellings are deserted, a few seats, destined to slowly disappear, make it look as if idle ghosts live there. In front of the others, the moment a ray of sunlight appears, the inhabitants settle into comfortable seats and watch cars—or, less often, walkers—go by. Needless to say, we're a big hit.

We set out at 8:00 a.m. from Pljevlja, quite late considering that a twenty-three-mile stretch lies ahead of us, starting with a mountain pass at an elevation of 1,260 meters (4,150 feet). Just outside town, the road overlooks a huge, open-air lignite quarry. The poor-grade coal it yields is used to fuel Montenegro's largest power plant, which went into service in 1982. The plant supplies a third of the country's electricity—and a great deal of pollution. A huge conveyor belt carries the waste material the plant generates to the top of the mountain, where it forms a massive black pyramid overlooking the landscape. As we're walking along one of the quarry's upper edges, a series of mines explode. Bulldozers immediately set about loading enormous trucks.

During our slow uphill climb, we're passed up by a hilarious couple, seemingly straight from a Kusturica film.* Sitting astride an out-of-breath moped is a fellow with windblown hair, and behind him, almost invisible, is a woman, squashed beneath the massive cast-iron stove she's hugging. Rising from the quirky couple, like the periscope of a strange submarine, is the stovepipe. A few yards on, the fellow has to stop to let the bike's overheated motor cool down. Just as our chances of winning this race of tortoises start looking reasonably good, the moped takes off again, coughing, misfiring, and spewing black-and-gray smoke. With the fatigue of the climb and my jubilation at this unexpected sight—a true gift on this luminous morn—I bungle the photo that would have preserved it forever. No matter: the image of that surreal scene is not something we will soon forget.

The Montenegrin customs officers, delighted to see French people, throw us a party. Things go rather differently on the Serbian side. A young official feeds our passports into his scanner, while warily looking us over. In a display of haughty indifference, which he no doubt thinks his job requires of him, he holds my passport loosely in the palm of his hand and strikes it with the stamp. The result is a perfectly illegible, blurry splotch of green ink, both for the name and the place. Another epic fail for my collection.

The sky doesn't give us much of a welcome either. The road climbs toward the pass until it reaches a white Orthodox church. A restaurant, the SOKO—meaning falcon—is a timely refuge, for a powerful

---

* TN: Born in Sarajevo, Yugoslavia, in 1954, Emir Kusturica is a filmmaker, actor, and musician.

storm strikes the border and a hailstorm blankets the ground in a carpet of white. The only customers this late for lunch, we stare out at the immaculate, silent mantle, which could just as well have been churned out by this little ski resort's snow guns.

We now need to come to a decision on the next chapter of our journey. I try explaining to Bénédicte that all wars are barbaric. Troops in the field, regardless of the side they're on, are rarely beyond reproach. We've learned how the atrocities committed by the Serbian, Croatian, and Bosniak armies and militias most often targeted civilians. They sought to "cleanse" the country of "others." Sometimes without sparing women, adolescents, the elderly, or even children. Absurd nationalism that somehow convinced them that they'd find peace by wiping away centuries of culture and history, that they could erase the pieces of the puzzle and invent for themselves brand-new religious purity.

Bénédicte, I can clearly tell, is still reluctant. There's no point in walking if our hearts aren't into it. So we'll take a bus to the city of Novi Pazar, a.k.a. "Little Istanbul," in anticipation of reaching the big one. From there, we'll return to our walk and head into Kosovo, covering in one fell swoop the equivalent of a four-day walk. In a sense, we're going to protest by climbing aboard a vehicle, whereas most protests—except for truck drivers (in trucks), farmers (on tractors), and cabbies (in taxicabs)—are accomplished on foot.

XV

A SERBIAN HIATUS

*Republic of Serbia (*Republika Srbija/РЕПУБЛИКА СРБИЈА*). Population: 7.7 million. Independence: 2006. Candidate for membership in the European Union since 2009.* Outside the Eurozone. Currency: the Serbian dinar (Srpski dinar). Capital city: Belgrade.*

In Prjepolje, the woman at the reception desk asks us to pay for the room right off the bat. Is it because she doesn't trust those without a car, who might also not have money? After seeing our room, we have another explanation: this is by far the filthiest hotel we've seen since setting out from Lyon. Despite the elevation, I find myself wondering whether we'd be better off camping.

Prjepolje is a bleak, poverty-stricken little town. Banks and betting shops almost outnumber cafes on Main Street, which also has, as in every Muslim-majority city, plenty of jewelry stores. In this community's wedding traditions, the groom must buy jewels and give them to his betrothed. In a way, it's insurance against divorce. The jewels become the spouse's dowry, and she gets to keep them in case there's a repudiation.

The city straddles the River Lim. On its very steep left bank, little white houses rise in tiers amid the greenery. After disassembling

---

* TN: Negotiations for Serbia's admission into the European Union began in 2014 and are ongoing; membership, however, will most likely not take place until at least 2025.

Ulysses and stowing him in his bag, we roam about to pass the time before boarding the bus that will carry us across Serbia. What a strange feeling. It's something that never happens with walking: pedestrians start and stop whenever they wish. With buses, motors control the clock.

Nearly all the men under forty have the same hairstyle: shaved sides and a long tuft slicked back over the top. It's a cut popular in West European countries as well, among young men. Was this innovative coif born here, or back home? Ah, the mysteries of fashion! While waiting to load Ulysses into the bus's belly, I reflect on our journey. I find that it has many positives. It has allowed me to grow closer to the woman I'm spending my life with. This is the first time in ages that Bénédicte and I have spent twenty-four hours a day together. And she has proven herself to be strong, attentive, brave, and so radiant that, whenever we interact with locals, they turn to her, not me. I remain ever in the background, a silent observer.

I had only a superficial awareness of the Balkans. The route we're traveling is quite the lesson in history and geography. Is there any better way to immerse yourself in a country than to walk across it, step by step? We get to know its geography through both our eyes and our calves. On that topic, we've now moved past the deep canyons and are entering a thickly forested zone; the road heads up some high hills in a series of wide switchbacks.

From Trieste on, I've been able to gauge the width and depth of the gulf separating the region's three communities. They butchered one another at the foot of each minaret and each steeple, and it sometimes seems like war is ready to flare up again, given how deep the hatreds run.

War. The atmosphere here has brought back distant memories. In Normandy, at the age of six, smack dab in the middle of the fighting that followed the Allied landings, I got to know what war was all about. I experienced the fear, the sound of the bombs, the frantic attempts of soldiers to escape gunfire, the sight of corpses—including an especially gruesome one, blackened by a flamethrower—and the angst triggered by the slightest sound of a tank or airplane engine. When the fighting was over, serenity triumphed. Here, we're occasionally gripped by the sense of an imminent threat, fueled by what we know of these Yugoslav Wars: the scars, the memories, the violence.

As we're exiting a cafe, a bearded young man jumps at the chance to practice the handful of English words he knows and asks us—this isn't the first time—whether there are jobs in France. Here, there aren't enough. Mihti's a chimney sweep, and everyone heats their homes with wood. Since very few city dwellers have enough room to store their wood for the winter, the poorly dried fuel they use dirties the chimneys, which must be swept every year. Unfortunately for Mihti, every household manages to cobble together a homemade brush. I suggest that he should start campaigning for the approach used in France: without a chimney sweep's certificate, if there's a fire, insurance companies won't pay. Since we're really getting into the conversation, I propose that we look for a table outside a cafe where we'll be more at ease to chat. I'd really like to better understand the relationship between Muslims, Catholics, and Orthodox Christians in Serbia. He first agrees, then seems to be looking for a spot where people would notice he's with foreigners; not finding one, he turns me down. So we part ways: I reach out my hand to say goodbye. Bénédicte does the same, but the fellow steps back, hides his right hand behind him, and says: "I'm Muslim and never shake hands with women." We feign surprise. What passage in the Qur'an forbids this simple and profoundly human gesture? He has no idea, but it's his right, of course, to do as he pleases, and he makes that clear. "Perhaps if Bénédicte were a close relative or friend," he says, "but she's a complete stranger!"

The next day, in Sjenica, we converse briefly with a young woman who tells us that she's not from here, she's staying only temporarily to study Serbian.

"What country are you from?"

"I'm Muslim."

We'll learn nothing more, since here, too, apparently, a religion can sometimes substitute for one's place of identity.

They slide Ulysses into the bus's baggage compartment, and off we go to Novi Pazar. The landscapes are magnificent. Forested hills in front of a high plateau, which, owing to the large number of ruminants, we nickname the "*plateau de mille mètres et de mille vaches*"—the Plateau of a Thousand Meters and a Thousand Cows.

The young woman referred to Novi Pazar as "Little Istanbul." Twenty years ago, this Raška-Province city had roughly equal numbers of Muslims and Orthodox Christians. But the war dramatically changed this equilibrium, and it did so even more in Kosovo. Scores of Serbs left, large numbers of Kosovars arrived, and today, Muslims account for about 80 percent of the population. Some believe that it's around here that problems are most likely to arise in the future. This evening, a large flock of young people is out strolling the city streets. The atmosphere of "Little Istanbul" is oppressive and we feel unwelcome. The moment we enter a cafe where there are only men, Bénédicte is subjected to looks of outrage and disapproval, and it infuriates her.

The room they rent us must measure at most six square yards, including just over one for the bathroom/toilet/shower, and the room's walls are so thin that, if we had neighbors, we could probably hear them breathe. We were planning on staying two nights, but in the morning, we check out with no regrets. Since we can't do anything about our souls, we head over to a laundromat and scrub our clothes clean.

Serbia is behind us. We're on our way to the country everyone has been warning us about: "Watch out for the mafia!"

XVI

KOSOVO: THE DIVIDING LINE BETWEEN COFFEE AND TEA

Kosovo (Kosovë). Population: 1.7 million. Independence: 2008. Albanian and Muslim majority, Serbian minority. Languages: Albanian, Serbian. Presence of multinational UN peacekeeping troops, known as KFOR (the Kosovo Force). Currency: the euro. Capital city: Priština.*

It's in Kosovo that the last of the Yugoslav Wars was fought. The Serbs, who saw the country as the cradle of their Christian culture, dreamed of including it in what they call "Greater Serbia." The Russians would later use a similar argument to destabilize and annex part of Ukraine. In 1990, two communities lived side by side: on one hand, Serbian Orthodox Christians, and on the other, Albanian-speaking Muslims, the majority, who wanted to declare their independence. In 1996, the Kosovo Liberation Army, or *UÇK (Ushtria Çlirimtare e Kosovës)*, was born. Under the leadership of Slobodan Milošević, the Serbian Army occupied the country. After the 1995 Srebrenica Massacre, the United Nations feared another campaign of ethnic cleansing. This time, they couldn't just stand idly by and do nothing. In 1999, the UN placed the country under its protection and demanded that Serbia end its repressions. When it was clear the

---

* TN: In 2018, KFOR consisted of approximately 4,000 troops.

United Nations' ultimatum would have no effect, NATO initiated a campaign of air strikes that would eventually force Milošević to concede.

Peace was restored, but it then had to be preserved. The UN created KFOR, a peacekeeping force whose job is to ensure that the two communities don't start fighting again. In 2008, Kosovo unilaterally declared its independence. But the tensions between Serbs and Albanians are so great that, as far as the future is concerned, there are no guarantees. The former still dream to some extent of "Greater Serbia," while the latter would welcome the formation of a "Greater Albania." Even today, the Serbs refuse to recognize Kosovo's independence. For them, the polity is merely a province of their own nation. On road maps sold in Serbia, no border is drawn between the two countries. Several Serbs we meet justify their claims to Kosovo by pointing out that there are Orthodox monasteries there, which the Muslims, they say, are destroying.

Përparim is a svelte fellow with a friendly face, visibly keen on interacting with passing foreigners. His perfect mastery of English facilitates our long conversations. He's forty-four. At eighteen, he fled his native Kosovo and the bombing. After a year in France, he continued on to England where his brother was living and remained there for seven more years, working as a baker, his father's profession. He then returned home, married a Kosovar, and today, he's the father of a little girl and works in Slovenia where wages are higher. That allowed him to build a house in his hometown.

The way he pictures Kosovo is, to say the least, sobering. The mafia is in control. In this country, he tells us, there are two million people and four million cars, most stolen from the EU. In any case, Europe and the United States provided the country with a great deal of financial assistance, but it's said that corruption diverted a large portion of the funds. Atop the rubble, after the massive air strikes of 1998 and 1999, new neighborhoods have been built. Today, the population is 80 percent Muslim, as compared with the 1980s, when Serbian- and Albanian-speaking communities were more or less equal. The departure of many Serbs in key positions necessitated rebuilding the national administration, the educational system, the police force, and the army.

Përparim is Muslim. That's what he told us anyway, and that's what he'll claim on the next national census. He has never set foot in a mosque and his only link to religion is the two-euro contribution he gives the imam each year, which will allow him, when he dies, to be buried for free. "Burial-blanket" coverage, if you will. But it's not so easy to escape from tradition. Our friend has worked a lot, often holding down two jobs at once, since, to pay for his wedding, he had to come up with twenty-five thousand euros. Six thousand went to buy gold jewelry for his fiancée. The rest was spent to sumptuously feed their four hundred guests. When we express how unfair that seems—at that price, there's no way poor people can ever marry—Përparim simply shrugs his shoulders: if he had done anything less, he would have lost face. One's social status and self-image are serious matters, not to be taken lightly.

Priština, the capital city, is one immense construction site. Roads are being built; tall, colorful high-rises are in the final stages of completion; and houses sprout like mushrooms from the ground—all, apparently, without any particular urbanistic concerns. "There's work for anyone who wants it here," Përparim tells us. The country's being rebuilt from the ground up. As soon as it was created, Kosovo adopted the euro. A workman earns four hundred euros a month ($530), a schoolteacher six ($800). The lunch we're having for three costs seven euros ($9.25). A cabbie offers to drive us to the Tirana Hotel, just outside the city. He'll be our guide. He wants three euros ($4) for the ride. Përparim has him wait for a full hour, while we talk. The driver doesn't mind a bit. When at last we climb into his vehicle, he stops at the first gas station and asks for two euros ($2.50), so we don't run dry. When we reach our destination, we hand him five euros ($6.60) for the ride. Surely the most he'll make all day.

"No coffee here, sir, only tea," we're told by the manager of the little bistro, where today, September 18, we enjoy an excellent breakfast.

We've no doubt just crossed over the dividing line between the land of coffee—omnipresent ever since we left Italy—and the kingdom of tea, which stretches all the way to Istanbul and China.

Out on the road, we descend into hell. If there are four million cars in Kosovo, we likely pass a good half of them that day. To exit Priština, we have to go through a kind of narrow bottleneck between a block of buildings and a cement wall. There isn't the slightest space or sidewalk where we can avoid cars, of which there are two lanes in both directions. Drivers notice us at the last moment, then veer mere inches away to dodge us without sideswiping the other line of moving vehicles. All with so much noise that we couldn't speak to one another if we wanted to. On two occasions, a truck has to stop to avoid hitting us. Once past the bottleneck, which must be about a mile and a quarter long, we have a tiny bit more room, but we're not out of danger yet. A four-by-four stops. It's an Englishman. He tells us that we're risking our lives and offers to take us on board. We thank him but turn him down. After a couple more incredibly tense miles, we finally find a parallel side road where we can safely walk. In the stream of vehicles, we notice several KFOR convoys go by, consisting of a dozen jeeps, some trucks, and an armored car.

The intense economic activity we noticed over the nineteen miles traveled that day is evidence of renewed economic strength. There's a long succession of workshops, commercial buildings, garages, and storage sheds. Selami, out in front of his brand-new aluminum-window factory, goes into wide-eyed shock the moment he spots our caravan, then invites us in for a drink of water. We gladly accept and settle comfortably into car seats arranged to create a sitting room in the middle of his shop. Selami began making his first windows just last week. He's twenty-seven years old and is clearly confident in his business's future, which employs two salaried workers. Out in front of his workshop, three flags wave in the wind: the American flag, the Kosovar flag, and the Albanian flag. He's Muslim and tells us that there were no atrocities committed by Serbs in large cities—in Priština and Frizaj—but that in villages, women and children were locked in houses, which armed men set on fire after they had shot everyone. The story's confirmed by Ismael, the manager of the hotel where we spend the night. He's quite fluent in French from having worked in Geneva for seven years, including six without papers. When his residence permit expired, he had to head home. Neither of them lost members of their immediate family in the war, but several friends and cousins were killed. I ask: "And what if the KFOR soldiers were to leave?" The question's not merely hypothetical: France is already in the process of withdrawing its soldiers.* "Not a good idea!" Ismael exclaims. "They had better stay for twenty years, or Kosovars will simply go back to fighting one another again."

A divine melody, unexpected amid all these roaring motors, drifts our way and softly caresses our ears. It's a flute and it's played by Ardan, a young, eighteen-year-old shepherd who, seated on the guardrail, is keeping watch over his goats as they graze beside the road. Amazed to hear such beautiful music in this odd location, Bénédicte asks him if she can make a recording. So the kid gives us an honest-to-goodness concert, overjoyed to have an audience of human ears. A few miles farther along, a cemetery belonging to the Kosovo Liberation Army, the *UÇK*, dominates the road, nicknamed the "Cemetery of Martyrs." Each black-granite tomb bears a photo: there are five women and about thirty men, the youngest of whom is eighteen and the oldest fifty. Each day, an Albanian flag is redrawn in the sand.

War is once again the topic of conversation at the Restaurant Beni, whose owner, Guri, became disabled when he was struck by three bullets. He tells us that the Kosovars purchased their weapons from Serbian soldiers. I've read elsewhere that a large share of the weapons used by the Kosovars came from Albania. Guri lived in Switzerland for eleven years before coming back home to start a business. He has researched the consequences of the war on a population of forty

---

* TN: In November 2013, France announced the departure of its 320 soldiers in Kosovo. They were progressively withdrawn over the course of the following year.

thousand. He claims that 687 houses were burned by the Serbs in his home region, and that 127 civilians and 87 soldiers died. Those who managed to get out fled to Germany, Switzerland, or France. After the war, humanitarian associations gave six thousand deutschmarks to each family so they could rebuild their houses. "People who lived under communism have a hard time understanding capitalism and miss the old days." As he sees it, the corruption in Kosovo is no worse than in France. "We have the best police force in all the Balkans. But as soon as someone, like me, builds a hotel, people think that it's with dishonest money." He also doesn't believe that diplomas can be purchased in his country. On the other hand, financial speculation is rampant. People who have the money hire others to build houses inexpensively for them, by employing Macedonian workers, for example. A day's work is paid ten euros ($13). The owners are convinced that, in three or four years, they'll be able to resell these houses for a killing. A risky bet, as Guri sees it. He did construction work on an eight-story apartment building in Priština. The building was completed three years ago, but so far, only one apartment has sold.

Shortly before the town of Kaçanik, Zija is waiting for us on the wayside. Yesterday, we lunched near the table he was seated at with his young wife, never guessing that the couple was intrigued by us. They left without trying to strike up a conversation. Zija's wife made him promise to find out more. The young man works with his father, who's a funerary monument maker. When he was between five and thirteen years old, he lived as a refugee in Germany, and is therefore fluent in the language. He also speaks a decent smattering of English. We decide to get a room in the dismal-looking Hotel Le Fontana, right across from where he lives, and we spend the evening in conversation with Zija and his friends. He openly shares his views with us. On education: "Public-school teachers are all communists." But he repeats what Guri told us: "Here, no one can buy a diploma." And his young wife, whom he married last month, is working very hard to earn hers. On the war: he didn't experience it personally and doesn't feel all that concerned. On young people: 10 percent of them are ready to wage jihad in Syria. Certain young men abandon their wives and children to go off and fight. In the city of Kačanik, there have already been five deaths. He's surprised that Syria is drawing so many to it, since very few went to Iraq. On salaries: people work eight hours a day, six days a week, for four hundred euros a month ($530). All families depend on the money those living abroad send back home. Zija sells a gravestone for between three and five hundred euros ($360–600), and nets between one and two hundred euros ($120–240). His brothers also work for the family business. On expenses: his fellow countrymen will give up anything in order to buy themselves a big car.

While we're chatting away, a Kosovar, accompanied by an African American, comes over to us. I ask a few questions of the American, who represents, he tells me, a humanitarian organization, although he refuses to say which one. He lives in Skopje, in Macedonia,* and is supposedly here on official "business." He refrains from saying more. In Kosovo, discretion is a form of life insurance.

Conversing with locals met by chance is always a joy, and I love it when destinies cross paths, but it's not always the best way to gain a clear understanding of the realities of a country. If that were the case, there'd be no corruption here, or at least "no more than in France"! On the way back to the hotel, I'll learn that three well-known Europeans who had been sent to Kosovo to assist in setting up the rule of law are currently on trial. Judges and prosecutors, they're accused of having accepted bribes after tipping the scales of justice in favor of Kosovars accused of serious criminal offenses. While the evil Serbs are denounced for having set houses on fire, their hosts, the good Kosovars, torched eight Serbian churches just as UN troops were arriving as reinforcements. In a war, no one is innocent.

The American we met yesterday forewarned us that the road leading out of Kaçanik is especially narrow, and so he advised us to get an

---

* TN: Known, since February 2019, as "North Macedonia."

early start to avoid traffic. He pointed out that there are several tunnels that would be extremely dangerous to travel through on foot, for they're narrow and unlit. One particularly helpful detail he shared is that, for the first two, the old road skirts the mountain. And indeed, at the entrance to the first tunnel, a small road appears off to our right, half overrun by weeds; we take it with short-lived glee. The spot has, in fact, become a dump cluttered with scrap metal, garbage, and, worst of all, rotting carcasses. Walking past a putrefying horse, we're asphyxiated by the stench, and almost find ourselves wishing we'd taken the tunnel. Along the little road we turn onto to avoid the following tunnel, the carcass of a cow, bloated like a balloon, is crawling with maggots. Just as fatigue is starting to get the best of us, one of Ulysses's tires goes flat.

In a few hours, we'll be crossing over into that country that you're no longer supposed to call Macedonia, but that everyone calls . . . you guessed it . . . Macedonia.

XVII

MACEDONIA

*Macedonia (*Makedonija/МАКЕДОНИЈА*).* Following a legal battle with Greece, which lays claim to the name "Macedonia," the country had to change its name to the "Former Yugoslav Republic of Macedonia," whose acronym is the FYRM. Population: 2 million. Religion: 64 percent Orthodox Christian, 33 percent Muslim. Alphabet: Cyrillic. Independence: 1991. The FYRM has been a candidate for entry into the European Union since 2004.† Currency: the Macedonian denar, pegged to the euro. Capital city: Skopje.*

Some claim that the country has a population of 1.8 million. Others put the figure at 2.1 million. Is there any way to know for sure? The government refuses to hold a census, which opens the door to a host of electoral manipulations. The opposition quips that there are 1.7 million *voters*. Even babies vote. And dead people.

A third of the country's population resides in Skopje, the capital. It's a nightmare trying to navigate since none of the road signs give clear directions. After a very long, grueling stretch that we have to finish up in the pouring rain, and saved when an employee of the

---

* TN: As previously mentioned, in February 2019, Macedonia officially became the "Republic of North Macedonia."

† TN: North Macedonia joined NATO in March 2020, the organization's thirtieth member state. Though North Macedonia has applied for membership in the European Union, Bulgaria, itself a European member state, has currently blocked negotiations due to a number of social and political disagreements it has with the country.

143

city's enormous American embassy puts us back on the right road, we finally reach a hostel, which at one time was for "youth."

It's Sunday: all the city is in the streets and especially in its churches. I'm surprised that a majority of those attending services are men, whereas in Catholic churches, you see mostly women. The crowds of men are almost as thick as in mosques for Friday prayer. At the entrance to the orthodox church, a woman is selling candles by the handful. She leaves her station from time to time to have a look around the sanctuary and collect any offerings left near the icons. In the evening, restaurants overflow with customers, and the music already has an Eastern ring to it.

Macedonia is no more immune from corruption than neighboring Kosovo. In May 2015, *Courrier International** tells me, a wiretap revealed that politicians close to those in power were taking bribes. In a country where the minimum wage is only 143 euros ($189) per month, this has the population quite angry. Another challenge the country faces is how to ensure the peaceful coexistence of Christian Macedonians (64 percent) and Muslim Albanians (33 percent).

In 1963, a massive earthquake wiped the country's capital off the map. It destroyed 80 percent of the city's dwellings and killed over one thousand people. During reconstruction, hundreds of statues, in classical Greek or Soviet style, sprung from the ground and invaded city squares, streets, and bridges. Some are gigantic. They evoke consensual themes such as solidarity, childhood, and motherhood, but none refer to the terrible natural catastrophe itself. The citizens of Skopje, who struggle to eke out a decent living, strongly protested these megalomaniacal expenditures.

Skopje's Contemporary Art Museum is worth the visit as much for what's on display as for the building itself, a former *han* (caravansary). I admire the skill of these architects who, in the absence of plate glass, found clever and elegant ways to channel natural light

---

* FN: *Courrier international*, a French weekly, publishes a selection of articles from newspapers and magazines around the globe, translated into French.

from the sky into these spaces, enclosed by high walls. Since the start of our journey, this is the first caravansary we've seen, which is proof that the Ottoman Empire left a strong imprint here.

Having set foot in the Macedonian capital, we've covered over half the distance from Verona to Istanbul. Three more days on our feet and we'll be leaving behind the countries of the former Yugoslavia, which were so violently and lastingly torn by war. Will Europe, itself so heterogeneous and poorly unified, succeed in effacing this hate-filled past and wash away all the spilled blood? From what I've seen, I doubt it. The hydra is only napping.

A bit wiser now after our difficult and interminable entry into this signless city, to get back out of Skopje, we take a taxi. Our driver's a former engineer who, tired of being under pressure from his job and boss, finally chucked it all. This morning, he can relax about his three-day-old beard and start work whenever he wants. He tells us that he's very happy like this. Is it that our conversation has distracted him, or has he given up reading signs altogether? He suddenly turns onto the little highway's exit ramp . . . in the wrong direction! A truck is coming straight at us. Neither party panics. Our driver keeps to the right, the other driver hugs the left guardrail, and both vehicles get through just fine.

He drops us off at the foot of a steep uphill section that will carry us to an elevation of 600 meters (2,000 feet) above sea level. Two solid hours of sweat, with Ulysses in tow. Six miles after Skopje, a massive garbage dump has us gasping for breath. There are so many abandoned pets in this country that not a day goes by without us stumbling upon the smelly carcass of a dog or cat, either tossed out onto the shoulder or simply left on the roadway where, flattened by hundreds of tires, all that remains is a furry spot on the pavement.

Each day, everything changes. Yesterday, in Skopje, the people we met spoke Serbo-Croatian (the ex-official Yugoslavian language). Today, in the little village of Nikuštak, people in the two bistros across from one another are conversing in Albanian. The one to our left is run by a fellow who worked in Switzerland for six years; he returned here, then bought himself a truck so that he could run deliveries. When he'd had his fill of that, he bought this bistro, where he blissfully spends his days conversing with customers. Everyone here is Muslim. Six miles down the road, the inhabitants are all Orthodox, and we don't see a single minaret. Here, there, no matter—they're all friendly.

Under an awning for protection from the sun, a man with translucent-blue eyes awaits customers. We deliver our usual spiel about our walk. He gets up and offers us a huge watermelon, which, as graciously as possible, we refuse, explaining that it's too heavy for Ulysses. In Kumanovo, where we find ourselves by mid-afternoon, a group of customers in a bar insists on paying for the tea we ordered the moment we walked in. One of them works in Switzerland. Another, a student, plans to go to Turkey where, he says, unemployment is non-existent.

The city of Kriva Palanka is surprisingly clean compared to those we've seen so far. There are even garbage cans. Straight off, of course, we ask a passerby whether he knows of a place where we could stay. Making plenty of gestures, he answers us in Macedonian/Albanian/Serbo-Croatian and, despite our obvious puzzlement, spews forth everything he has to say until there's nothing left. But two passing students now happily realize that they've come upon an opportunity to make use of the German they're learning. They're joined by three men who were observing us from a shop, and they, too, get in on the conversation, speaking English. It's Babel revisited. After a few minutes, we manage to sort things out: there is indeed a hotel here but, they tell us, it would be much better if we went another kilometer down the road to a monastery near the Bulgarian border by the name of Joakim Osogovski. So off we go.

It will take us not one, but six or seven kilometers to get there. At the end of a steep climb, we discover an Orthodox church, a chapel, and several conventual buildings clinging to a rock wall; they rise above the sheer cliffs of a narrow canyon, at the bottom of which sings a rushing mountain stream.

From the monastery, the view of the valley grows even more beautiful when a ray of sunlight breaks through the torrential rains of the past two days. Not a single square inch of the church's walls is free of paintings, both inside and out. Biblical scenes, sublime-faced cherubs flying about here and there, icons of saints; and violent images too, of decapitations and bodies harshly thrashed by swords and spears. It's a stunning display. As in most Westerns, it's easy to tell the good guys from the bad: the former have pale skin and haloes, the latter, horned and painted black, are either bathed in blood or burning in the flames of hell. The inscriptions are all in Cyrillic. A representation of the Last Supper depicts seven apostles only, seated around the figure of Christ. The iconostasis presents two mirror images of Saint Michael, but no Satan. There is a beautiful representation of God the Father in Majesty in the exterior gallery. A place like this makes quite clear what differentiates Orthodox Christians from Muslims, who reject the use of icons.

The only thing monastic about the room they give us is the sobriety of its furniture. It has a magical view of the church and valley, a bathroom with no leaks, clever lighting, and is impeccably clean. Full of peaceful beauty and silence, the place immediately perks us up. It's beyond a doubt the most beautiful room we've stayed in since setting foot in the Balkans. And it costs just ten euros per person.

For dinner, finding the monastery's restaurant unexpectedly closed, we have instant soup in our room. It will have to sustain us well into tomorrow. In the morning, we set out on empty stomachs, warmly dressed to protect ourselves from the cold, wet air. Two closed restaurants and two hours later, we're thrilled to find Lily, stamping her feet to stay warm in a sunny spot of the road. Her restaurant is set up on the wayside. It's a camper with its wheels removed and serves both as food stand and kitchen. A taut tarp functions as a covered patio: for us, shivering and dreaming of coffee and breakfast for nearly three hours now, it's a veritable five-star hotel. Lily is the same age as Bénédicte but looks ten years older. She proudly tells us about her twenty-six-year-old daughter who lives in California, and whose life will be better than hers. Cold weather is on its way. She'll soon lock up her roadhouse and head back to the city, where she'll try to find a job for the winter. There's a great weariness in her eyes. I pay for our coffees by emptying my pockets of all the denars I can find, for they'll be of no use to me in Bulgaria. When she counts the coins, her wide smile tells me that it will be her sale of the day. We get going again with the little cakes she insists on giving us. Thank you, Lily.

The border doesn't come easy. It's located at 1,100 meters (3,600 feet) above sea level.

* * *

Skopje, Macedonia—September 21: Our 8th Border Crossing

Not only did the Serbs not chop off our heads, but the first Serbian city we came to—nicknamed "Little Istanbul"—was teeming with Muslims!

There goes the neighborhood . . .

With its gloomy, inhospitable feel, we didn't linger for long in Novi Pazar. I had the distinct feeling that women were very unwelcome in cafes, when all the men's eyes turned my way as if to say: "And just what do you think you're doing here, little lady?"

The day before that, too, a fellow who called out to us in the street, all too happy to practice his English with a couple of foreigners, refused to shake my hand, claiming that doing so was against the Qur'an. Well, isn't that grand: do I smell bad, or what? I don't know what it is that makes them so sectarian—religion or culture—but gender equality here? I wouldn't hold my breath!

In short, we're happy to have made it to Kosovo where the atmosphere is cheerful and lively. We had been warned that this was a nasty country, full of ruffians, but the people we've met are both charming and hospitable, much more extroverted than elsewhere, probably because there are a lot of young people and emigration has long been a way of life here, and consequently, English and French are widely spoken (some Kosovars made their fortunes in Switzerland).

Now that peacetime is finally here, people are in a hurry to be happy.

Përparim, Guri, Ismaël, Selami, Zija, and the others: they all spoke to us at length about their country, their aspirations, and—for those that experienced it—the war.

Ten thousand victims. It was about time NATO woke up.

Even today, KFOR—the Kosovo Force—is everywhere. Now that they're safe, people can legitimately hope for a better future. In any case, that's what they're doing, judging from the hundreds of buildings going up along with the trash bins that go with them, and which are turning Priština's vast plain into an endless garbage dump.

Two million inhabitants, four million cars. They're everywhere, Mercedes first and foremost, but Ferraris, too. There's trafficking galore and corruption is thriving. On the other hand, 50 percent of young people are unemployed, and a typical twelve-hour day brings a worker just ten euros ($13). Still, they're ready to starve themselves if that's what it takes to buy the Mercedes of their dreams, and they'll blow twenty thousand euros to get married with all the bells and whistles. I don't get it.

Kosovo is an extension of Albania, and many would like Albania to annex Kosovo one day.

We put our Bosnian/Serbo-Croatian back on the shelf; it's time for us to learn Albanian!

We drop "Dobar dan" and start saying "Mirëdita" (hello).

In Serbia, the men are chiseled-bodied giants; their noses are shaped like the prows of overturned ships, and, like sails, must catch a lot of wind. Kosovar men, on the other hand, are rounder, softer, shorter; they have more attractive, jovial faces and twinkling eyes. We're back to the Mediterranean, and the optimism that prevails here is delightful. Let's hope the future proves them right.

Kosovars have such a keen sense of comfort that they can make even the most pitiful wayside patio feel homey. Gas stations are the clear winners at roadside "coziness": they have sofas and soft, colorful pillows, the kitschiest fountain imaginable, little trees and they're not even made of plastic. That's the patio at the Esso station and the BP station sofa, where we take delightful naps.

Little by little, the Orient is starting to rub off on us.

I haven't got much to say about the women since we don't see any. In cafes, "ne"; *in restaurants, all the servers are men; they're the ones out buffing cars for sale as well or managing the numerous scrapyards. It's men who drive the trucks and tractors, men who work in the fields.*

---

* TN: "No," in Serbian, is "*ne*"; the most common Albanian form is "*jo*."

The women, of course, are indoors, and we're out. We miss them.

For the walker, happiness is . . . a SIDEWALK!

Especially when looming ahead is one of those cursed four-lane high-ways that can't be avoided when traveling in or out of large cities.

And then the sidewalk abruptly disappears, along with all the joy.

Taking a deep breath, we grit our teeth and venture out onto the roadway, and to hell with the trucks brushing past us: I go first, while Bernard brings up the rear with Ulysses, who has to stay behind, since, if he were to be hit by a car, he'd be transformed into a rather deadly catapult.

I never thought I'd do anything like that! But with Bernard, nothing is impossible.

Even walking through tunnels.

For Bernard is THE KING OF THE ROAD!

In tunnels, you have to have a sidewalk. No sidewalk, no tunnel.

It's never wide enough, in which case we have no choice but to hold up Ulysses's right wheel, keeping it suspended in mid-air.

Most terrifying of all is reaching a section where the lightbulbs have all burned out.

That's DARKNESS, real DARKNESS!

And it's scary as hell.

The last tunnel we took was just 140 yards long, so Bernard decided to make a mad dash between two cars from one end to the other! He took off like a bat out of hell: I ran after him as best I could, roaring with laughter. That man never ceases to amaze me.

In Skopje, we tasted our first meze and piroshka, and, everywhere we go, yogurt.

BF

XVIII

BULGARIA

Bulgaria (Republika Balgariya). Population: 7.2 million. Religion: mostly Orthodox Christian. Alphabet: Cyrillic. Member of the European Union since 2007. Outside the Eurozone. Currency: the Bulgarian lev. Capital city: Sofia.

With Ulysses in tow, we endured a four-hour struggle to reach the Bulgarian border. As usual, the trucks that passed us on the way up now wait their turn to get through customs. Throwing them smug little smiles, we overtake all these mastodons and shamelessly cut in front of them. Of course, none of the drivers protest, curiosity winning out over any concerns about who got there first. I hand our passports to the Macedonian customs agent who, pursing his lips with the two documents in hand, gapes in amazement as Bénédicte plants Ulysses right in front of the first eighteen-wheeler. Walkers get to enjoy a few simple pleasures every now and then, too.

His counterpart on the Bulgarian side is less interested in our passports than in our cart. Having looked it over from wheels to tow bar, he hands me back our two passports and waves us on. But the stamps?! I protest, I want the stamps! He kindly obliges and laughs outright when he learns where we're from and where we're going. Customs agents get to enjoy their share of simple pleasures, too.

We begin the long descent to Kyustendil after filling up on water at a gushing spring. Bulgaria, famous for its thermal and mineral springs, is said to have six hundred of them. After a two-hour

152

downhill stretch, I wander off to photograph a peasant farmer astride some kind of soapbox-derby cart pulled by a donkey, a vision from another age. Upon my return, I find Bénédicte beside herself: Ulysses's tow bar has snapped. Without that tube, our wagon can't be steered. I try improvising a temporary fix by lashing a branch to it, but that lasts only ten yards. We'll need to do a weld. We have no choice but to hitch a ride to the nearest garage. But it's no use, none of the cars even pretends to slow down. I go over to a woman farmer and ask: "taxi?" She launches into a monologue interspersed with grand gestures, then turns her back to me. I try again with a man who, outside his front door, is playing with a shaggy little red-furred dog that's prancing about between house and yard. He replies with a gesture that I take to mean "My poor old man! There's nothing I can do for you!" but then, in a change of heart, pulls a cell-phone from his pocket. He extends an invitation to us: *"Kafe?"*—A cup of coffee? Why not! Above Valentin's door, a large sign proclaims "COFFEE / BAR." Business was poor and he had closed up his shop, but he doesn't seem too upset, and won't let us pay. A photo, arm in arm with Bénédicte, will suffice. Soon after, the taxi arrives. It's a Fiat 500 and, with our bags and Ulysses, I doubt we'll fit. But Vasil, the driver, a big cool-headed fellow with no doubts whatso-ever, manages to squeeze all our gear into his tiny vehicle, then has us climb aboard too. Vasil, having lived for six years in Leonardo da Vinci's homeland, speaks fluent Italian. Bénédicte, delighted that she doesn't have to rack her brains with the handful of Serbo-Croatian words she knows—that hasn't happened since Trieste—makes his acquaintance and asks a few ad hoc questions so we can have our cart repaired as soon as possible. After a stop to see a friend of Vasil's who repairs bicycles but can't do anything for Ulysses, we pull up at Boyan's house. We find him busy welding beneath a large German car. Welding is exactly what Ulysses needs. While Bénédicte goes off with Vasil in search of a hotel for the night, Boyan repairs Ulysses's tow bar, having raised him up like a limousine on a metal lift. All the while, Boyan explains that his son is a math professor in a university in the United States, in South Carolina. A half-hour later, Ulysses is as good as new, and it costs us next to nothing.

That evening, we realize that, upon crossing the border, we entered a new time zone. I add an hour to my watch.

Cutting across the city of Kyustendil is a very wide pedestrian avenue, a tree-lined boulevard flanked with cafes, sidewalk terraces, gardens, movie theaters, and a playhouse. All the city's streets connect to this promenade. Just one lets cars cross over to the other side of this peaceful haven, where people stop, chat, and savor their cups of coffee. You could easily think you were in a Spanish city at the hour of the *paseo*, when the temperature drops and conversations resume.

Tomorrow, we're planning a side trip to visit Rila, one of the most famous monasteries in Bulgaria and the Balkans. Foot travel and tourism do not always mix, as each curiosity comes at the cost of added long walks. But the marvel people have told us about is far too tempting. We'll take a bus to Rila, for, to go there on foot, we'd need a full week.

At an elevation of 1,200 meters (4,000 feet), Rial is an architectural jewel in the middle of an immense forest. In the year 875, King Boris the First of Bulgaria abandoned Bogomilism, a religious movement rather close to Catharism. In France, the Catholic Church would combat the Cathars, a fight that took an especially fierce turn during the Albigensian Crusade (1209–29). I recall Arnaud Amaury's famous reply, captain of the army laying siege to the city of Béziers, when he heard that some of the prisoners were claiming to be Catholic: "Slay them all!" he said. "God will recognize his own!" Boris the First, having converted to Christianity, abdicated to become a monk. But, seeing that his son Vladimir, who had succeeded him, was attempting to return to the former religion, he did not turn the other cheek. He deposed him, had his eyes gouged out, and handed power over to another of his sons.

The Orthodox version of Christianity gained a foothold in Rila when, in the tenth century, a hermit decided to make his home here, with "the rock for my bed, the sky for my shelter."* So he established a monastery, which thrived and was eventually fortified with high walls. In times of danger, the monks would take refuge in the square tower at its center. The site became a Christian sanctuary in a mostly Muslim region and would remain so until the fall of the Ottoman Empire. In the nineteenth century, the buildings were destroyed by fire but were rebuilt true to the originals. Today, the monastery is a UNESCO World Heritage site.† There are no crowds, for coming here to pray requires considerable effort. After changing buses three times, we now stand at the entrance, a veritable castle gate. Thick as it is, it could surely hold back an entire army. The three-story-tall buildings form a paved quadrangle, planted with tall trees. Each floor looks out onto the courtyard through a covered gallery. In the middle rises a four-domed church and the tower. The stones, which are enormous, are painted black and white for the living quarters, and black and red for the church. The latter structure is covered inside and out with vivid paintings for the edification of the faithful. Heaven, God, angels in pure white robes, and demons, black with bat-like wings: those are some of the images covering the walls. The demons lure human beings to them by brandishing bags of gold, then drag them off to Hell by their feet. The angels, with swan-like wings and faces that are, well . . . angelic . . . but also impassive, run the demons through with long pikes. The church's interior is surprisingly lavish. To lure human beings in, do the monks use the shimmer of old gold, too? The chandeliers, as well as the chains they hang from, are made either of gold or gilded metal; the saints' haloes are of solid silver. The priestly vestments are woven of silk and gold. How did this place, established by a man who had renounced all earthly possessions,

---

* TN: Ollivier is referring to St. Ivan of Rila here, also known as John of Rila, patron saint of Bulgaria, and one of the most prominent saints of the Orthodox Church. The quotation is from the Testament of St. John of Rila (dated 941). Jonathan Dunne translates the Bulgarian as "the sky was my shelter, the earth was my bed."

† TN: The designation was made in 1983.

become such a vault of valuables? And the word is not too strong, for, at nightfall, the heavy, reinforced doors are carefully bolted shut. We are astonished yet again by the conduct of the faithful. Three successive signs of the cross as they enter the holy place, then three more in front of an icon protected by a pane of glass, which they kiss with their lips and forehead. Then a second icon, more signs of the cross, and more kisses. When they leave, the faithful walk backwards, making numerous signs of the cross, always in the Orthodox manner: hand to the right shoulder, then to the left. Orthodox Christianity is a religion of symbols, and of gold.

At our arrival, a monk wrapped in a long, dark robe and wearing a black hood over his head, in front of which a silk veil has been pinned, rents us a cell for the night. "Rents" isn't quite the right word. The holy man has us sign a contract stipulating that, since we're on a spiritual journey, we would like to donate sixty lev ($40) to the monastery, the price of a good hotel room. The room is monastic, and a large leak in a pipe has turned the bathroom floor into a footbath. Instead of a heater, there's a large pile of blankets. Thank goodness too, for, by morning, given the altitude, the temperature in the cell drops to nearly forty degrees Fahrenheit, even in summer. It seems that the Orthodox Church is suffering a vocations crisis, too, for over the course of nearly twenty-four hours, we encounter just three monks.

As we're leaving Rila early the next morning, Jo, a young American who looks a bit like Jesus, tells us that he's doing his grand European tour this year. A cancer researcher, he wants to travel to France to learn French and work for *Médecins sans frontières*, those "French doctors." He's plans on settling in the city of Le Lavandou on the French Riviera for a while, where he'll be "WWOOFing"— volunteering on an organic farm in exchange for room and board.[*]

In the villages we traverse, in front of the little houses, trellises are heavy with grapes, forming tempting cordons on either side of the streets.

---

[*] TN: World-Wide Opportunities in Organic Farming.

The little town of Samokov is perched at 950 meters (3,100 feet) above sea level. The surrounding summits are already powdered with snow. The region is known for its "Seven Lakes," which rise in tiers between 2,000 and 2,500 meters (6,500 and 8,000 feet). In the summer, it attracts droves of hikers, but right now, there's a winter chill in the air. It's time we start protecting ourselves from the cold, which will be with us now all the way to the plains of Turkish Thrace. Ski hats and gloves in our pockets, we tour the town. It once boasted twelve mosques. We find only one, and it's locked. We dine by the light of a wood fire at the excellent Hotel Sonata. The owner's wife speaks a few words of French, and her husband can mutter a bit of English. At breakfast, Bénédicte receives a lesson in the comparative linguistics of Bulgarian and English from Petia, the waitress. She's married to a Brit and is perfectly bilingual. Before getting back underway, we congratulate our hosts on their establishment, which we've just named "best hotel" beyond Trieste.

* * *

Plovdiv, Bulgaria—October 2

Our ninth border post, fourth language, and fifth currency.

And everywhere we look, minarets and domes, one after the other, and all muddled up in the landscape.

We no longer know who is who, who speaks what, who believes in whom, or who pays in what.

Our heads are spinning.

We let our footsteps guide us and they lead us ever eastward, with the sun in our eyes each day till noon.

After that, it rains. Often.

In Macedonia, we say goodbye to the Mercedes and limousines, and hello to all the faded red Yugo 45s and no-go Ladas.

As in Kosovo, life unfolds peacefully, without having to lose it to earn one.

The day at hand will be what it will be.

On the road, we encounter a great deal of kindness and solicitude. One man offers us a watermelon with a smile that says, "don't go!" Another screeches to a halt in his Yugo for a photo op with us.

Arid, worn-down hills—northern Macedonia resembles Corsica, but even the Corsican Department of Transportation is faster and more efficient than the DOT here, where road-clearing operations involve four people, a shovel, and a bottle. The shovel's for the fellow clearing the road; the bottle, so that the other two can booze it up.

The two places are alike in terms of road signs, too. Sometimes "ima" (there are some). And sometimes "nema" (there are none). Such as in Skopje (the capital city, no less), where we had such a tough time finding our way downtown that we took a taxi to get back out. The driver—a rather philosophical ex-engineer who had a habit of driving the wrong way down four-lane-highway off-ramps (why not?)—suggested that, for the road signs, we should come back in ten years. But we won't be coming back, Skopje's too ugly.

Going from one country to the next always takes place at a high point in the terrain. We know we'll first have to climb (up to 1,400 meters when going from Bosnia to Montenegro), then do a long downhill stretch to the next city.

Border crossings make me nervous. I have dreadful memories of those in former Soviet Europe, back when an East German customs officer could make you unload every piece of stage decor off the truck, then load it all back on again, just to be annoying. He had the power to do it, so he did.

And then, thanks to Schengen, it's easy to get used to moving freely about!

Still, since Slovenia, we've met only good-natured customs officers. I should point out that we're very much the main event at these little border posts, which are often little more than rickety portacabins (with couches and TV sets, nonetheless).

The customs agent standing guard outside alerts the second-in-command that there's a couple of Francuskis with an odd-looking bicycle. The second-in-command steps out, snatches our passports from the lookout's hands, notifies the commander on the sofa who climbs out of it to see what all the fuss is about. In short, everyone in the portacabin steps out, each with something to say in French or English, either out of admiration or incredulity. They let us know where we'll find the nearest cafe or drinking fountain, then turn around and return inside to escape the sun or warm back up.

Bernard, who has his own unpleasant memories of customs agents— Asian, in his case—always clamors for them to stamp his passport. And woe to those who forget or can't be bothered to make sure the mark is legible!

We're not going anywhere until we get the stamp!

The first few times, I tugged on his sleeve and whispered: "Come on, let's just go!" for the best customs office is the one you've put behind you. But then I realized that the fellows were actually quite happy to give us our souvenir stamps.

So our passports are now full of them.

Bulgaria's off to a bad start . . . and a good start. Ulysses's tow bar broke six miles beyond the border post, out in the middle of nowhere. We were stranded.

But breaking down offered an opportunity to meet some wonderful people: Valentin, who phoned a cab for us after our attempts at hitchhiking fell flat; then Vasil, who, thank goodness, spoke Italian, and took us straight to a mechanic, Boyan, a kind man with big bright eyes who welded, drilled, and sawed in just the right places to get Ulysses up and running again. With all the commotion, we lost our map and, unfortunately, Google Maps lost us, too. Whether we had entered a dead zone or a black hole, the area was "unavailable." Explanation unknown. So we really need to get our hands on a map.

This time, the Latin alphabet is gone for good, and we have to start deciphering Cyrillic. Bernard jumps right in with the Russian he remembers from his Silk Road days, while I do a quick study of the new polite phrases and expressions we'll need to survive.

Bulgarians are not as jovial as Kosovars (although they're undoubtedly less scheming!); they're also shorter and chubbier. And much less considerate on the road, where we get yelled at and pushed from behind by morons ready to pass us up at any old place. It's terribly unpleasant!

The time has come for me to start using the "bras d'honneur."* Aaaaaaaah!

Bulgaria is a land of trellises, wine, monasteries (including fabulous works of art hidden up in the mountains), tripe soup and sheep's milk cheese (yum!), but above all, it's home to those world-famous Bulgarian voices, a musical genre that I fell head over heels for over twenty years ago.

By some incredibly serendipitous twist of fate, of dates and of people, we were able to attend one of their concerts in a small mountain village's community banquet hall. A Bulgarian soccer club was playing the Real Madrid that same evening, so the room was half empty: you can't compete with soccer!

All the old feelings came rushing back: I had shivers from head to toe. I felt as if the women were singing just for me.

After all, to hear them, I had come over 1,500 miles on foot!

---

* TN: a.k.a. the Italian salute.

We put our legs through a crash-test: thirty miles and two flat tires, the last at around six in the evening, that fateful hour when daylight beats a retreat, and we urgently need to find a room for the night. Flat tires always seem to happen when you're in a hurry, don't they? Let me just say that Bernard is quick on the draw when it comes to patching a tire or replacing an inner tube.

Who needs Le Mans? It's the "Twenty-Four Hours of the Balkans" every day here!

Of course, we were a rather pitiful sight the following day, with a twenty-two-mile stretch to get to Plovdiv.

Sometimes we think we're not capable, then, out of necessity, we manage it and realize that we are in fact perfectly capable.

Our bodies are growing stronger, we're building stamina. Each stride comes easily now; my tendonitis is all but forgotten.

For Bernard, stamina is an intrinsic part of who he is. Like Obélix, he fell into the magic potion when he was just a little tyke, back when he had to do a seven-and-a-half-mile round trip twice a day in clogs, his feet half frostbitten, just to get to school.

That, plus ten years of marathons, and the 8,700 miles he walked in his sixties—if that won't strengthen your calves, nothing will!

We're in good health. Not even a touch of turista these past two months. What we're eating is both a pleasure for the palate and good on the gut. You don't realize it until you have to settle for a disgusting frozen pizza, which happened only once. As far as the food here is concerned, French restaurants can eat their heart out.

We've been living and walking side by side "00–24" as it's written on motel-room doors—twenty-four hours a day—and in closer proximity than we've ever had to before, given our busy schedules. But despite the challenges we face, the doubts, the fatigue, and the bouts of morning blues, we still haven't squabbled. It's a little suspicious!

Will this team hold up all the way to Istanbul?

You'll find out in the next episode!

BF

* * *

From Samokov to Kostenets, we travel twenty-four miles over a rocky road on which ascents to over 1,100 meters (3,600 feet) alternate with nosedives into deep valleys. At the Hotel Diani, where we dine, we talk with the server, a young woman who's delighted to make use of her excellent English, which she learned by taking correspondence courses and watching television. Bénédicte happens to mention how she absolutely adores those world-famous Bulgarian women's choirs and asks whether any concerts might be taking place along our route. The young woman bursts out laughing: these women, for whom singing is like breathing—she bumps into them every day, they're her neighbors! And it just so happens that a free public concert is taking place this very night. Any idea where? Right here in Kostenets, only two hundred yards away! It just started. Waiting for dessert now out of the question, Bénédicte dashes off to fetch her recorder. Ten minutes later, we're seated in the concert hall, spellbound. Dressed in traditional costumes, the women blend their voices in a very special way. They are thirty or forty colorful nightingales who, full of infectious joy, propel the notes they sing high into the skies while our enraptured souls hang on for dear life and fly right up there with them. Bénédicte is moved to tears. Sadly, the concert is already almost over, which leaves us quivering . . . and frustrated. In the lobby, overcome with emotion, we corner one of the singers, Ralitsa, who informs us that on October 1, the troupe will be giving a concert in . . . Samokov, the city we set out from this very morning. Bénédicte is beside herself. It's September 27, and while we could possibly sacrifice a day or two, we'd have a hard time sitting still for five. We have to push on. We head to bed thrilled at having seized this extraordinary opportunity.

The following day, we embark on a very long thirty-mile hike. Our muscles are battle hardened; yes, we're sometimes plagued by pains, but at this point, we're confident that we can make it to the finish line. The weather is favorable: an overcast sky, mild temperatures, and terrain that, if not level, is at least not nearly as uneven as the chain of mountains we just crossed. Ever since Bénédicte's forced time off, we've been extremely reasonable: short stages, maximum hydration, regular rest stops. So it's time we put ourselves through the "crash-test," as Bénédicte calls it, somewhat puckishly, her head still in the stratosphere from yesterday's concert. She tells me how she first discovered Bulgarian choirs long ago, back when everyone was still listening to music on 33-rpm discs. Immediately hooked, she bought every recording she could find of those birds of paradise, and even adapted the polyphonic masterpieces for two voices, one being her own. There's simply no getting the Samokov concert off our minds. It isn't long before we figure out how to work it into our schedule. I dial up the hotel in Samokov and ask to speak to Petia; she confirms for us that there is indeed a concert scheduled for October 1. We ask her to reserve two seats for us, which she's happy to do. The restaurant's owners front the money for us. We'll forge ahead with our walk all the way to Plovdiv, Bulgaria's second-largest city, where we had planned a day off. We'll take a bus from Plovdiv back to Samokov so that we can be there for the October 1 concert without falling too far behind on our walking schedule. While we still have her on the phone, we ask Petia to book a room for us at the Hotel Sonata, which, at this point, is our absolute favorite. Bénédicte, over the moon at the thought that she'll soon be seeing her idols again, now floats over the pavement as she walks along.

After setting out a seven in the morning, we reach Pazardzhik at half-past seven in the evening, with daylight fading fast, in a state of utter exhaustion. Ulysses's left tire flatted twice—I had to repair it on-site, for I always have one spare inner tube, but not two. The pain in my thigh started acting up on several occasions, probably just to keep me from forgetting that I am, after all, an old man, but my endorphins kicked in each time, and I'm still able to walk without too much pain. Bénédicte also made it through the ordeal. Seventy-eight miles in three days: not bad for the walking wounded! We have seventeen miles to go before Plovdiv.

The next day, after yesterday's feat, getting going again is a real struggle. Our pains immediately flare back up. And the road is deadly dangerous. It has just two lanes, but Bulgarian drivers act as if there were three. The danger's made far worse by the presence of roadside grape vendors. Each autumn in Bulgaria, people busy themselves with some perfectly illicit "cooking": they transform apples or grapes and a bit of sugar into a very strong alcohol—fully 140-proof—known as *rakiya*. Farmers pile up fifty-kilo sacks of fruit, which customers drive off with in their trunks. Is fraud so common-place here that there's no point in doing this on the sly, or do the authorities simply look the other way? On several occasions, a driver, having spotted sellers off the road behind the undergrowth, slammed on the brakes and nearly caused a pile-up, with us as its first victims. On this straight, flat road, we actually wouldn't have been the first, for a good dozen lives have already met their end here, summed up today by little altars that the families erect for a daughter, a son, a husband, a father. There are many of them, and the objects they incorporate reflect either the means or the beliefs of the departed's family or friends: a photo etched in stone (we even find three mem-bers of the same family on one plaque), a perpetual flame, a variety of crosses, flower beds, tables and benches, cement edging. So many painful stories, some accompanied by photos, such as this one here of a young, handsome teen, proudly seated on the hood of a red German car. And on the grass nearby, a twisted fragment of the scar-let car that killed him. Others feature a steering wheel or rim. These post-mortem monuments have, however, no value at all as deterrents, for drivers on the adjacent road fearlessly speed up as they go past, so as not to miss their meeting . . . or their rendezvous with death.

The local Highway Department had the excellent idea of planting both sides of the road with different tree species, roughly a new one every six miles: walnuts, weeping willows, birches, lindens, plane trees. But they forgot to maintain them. Shrubs consequently grow out toward the road until, too close, they're clipped by passing cars.

The upper branches, meanwhile, are pruned by trucks. It looks as if someone had sculpted a green hat into this curtain of foliage, which shivers with each passing vehicle. And beneath the hat, there's the two of us, on pins and needles, with no shoulder where we can sidestep danger. So we walk on the roadway, facing the speedsters, some noticing us at the last moment. But it gets worse. When there's the slightest lull in the oncoming traffic, impatient drivers seize the opportunity to pass. We're caught unawares since they come up on us from behind. On a couple occasions, the car passing us brushed past us at over sixty miles per hour. That same day, after a truck nearly touched my elbow, we stood in silence for several minutes, trying to catch our breath. Are we, too, going to wind up memorialized on one of these wayside altars?

The road is a marketplace. In the villages, farmers and Romany vendors sell watermelons. Hanging from the walls are chili peppers, onions and shallots, green melons, and peppers, both yellow and red. In front of people's homes, wood is being stacked up in advance of winter, which is already in the air. At an intersection, some cops are watching us from a distance. There are three of them, lined up, more or less blocking the way, with their eyes glued on us, while completely ignoring the anarchic traffic. Is this going to be our first police check? As we draw near, one of them rushes over to the trunk of their patrol car and pulls out two bottles of cool mineral water, which the trio hands us with big smiles on their faces.

Making our way into Plovdiv is hard work. Ulysses, just like us, hates the old city's large, round cobblestones. The youth hostel has been closed for three years, we're told. The charming woman at the reception desk of a nearby *pansion* (boarding house) rents us a room; she also offers to do our laundry. I head off in search of some puncture-repair patches, for Ulysses's tires are leaking dangerously again, and I've exhausted my supply. An old man in the far back of an odds-and-ends shop talks me into a box of fifty; he doesn't do retail. Though it's mild out, we've burned through so many calories that when we sit down to eat, we're shivering. Some hearty soup, a steamy shower, and a lazy morning in bed until 8:30 get us back on our feet.

Plovdiv is beautiful and clean. Squads of female workers sweep the streets early in the morning, cobblestone by cobblestone, and everyone does a little cleaning outside their own door. Here again, richly decorated Orthodox churches stand shoulder to shoulder with mosques, one of which, during the Ottoman period, was the largest in all the Balkans. It's magnificent. The Old City is sublime, with timbered houses and corbelled upper floors. They're all colorfully painted. Lamartine stayed in one of them on his *Voyage en Orient*.* Climbing the steep hill in terraces, these houses form a showcase for a remarkably well-preserved Roman theatre. A little farther below, one can tour the ruins of an ancient stadium that measured 380 feet long, and which could accommodate thousands of spectators.

On the immense central square, reminiscent of Soviet design, we get to know Petko, a retired engineer, who tells us that he once made regular trips to Paris where he tirelessly strode the length and breadth of the city's first five arrondissements. His daughter Martina, a journalist, worked there for a time. She's now a New York correspondent for the Bulgarian national television network's Channel Two, and he's extremely proud of her. Her son's a painter and is finishing up his studies. We visit a gallery where his artwork is on display alongside that of ten or so other artists. Petko confirms our hunch that gallery space is hard to come by, for over 450 painters live in the city, more than anywhere else in Bulgaria.

Alexander I Avenue has a Mediterranean feel to it. It's where people go, starting about 6:00 p.m., to see friends and to be seen. The

---

* TN: Alphonse de Lamartine (1790–1869) was a French statesman involved in the establishment of the Second Republic, as well as an author, poet, and Orientalist. He was an early advocate of vegetarianism. In 1835, he published *Voyage en Orient* (*Travels in the East*), which tells of a journey he took in 1832–33 to Lebanon, Syria, and the Holy Land along with his wife Elisa (a painter and sculptor herself) and ten-year-old daughter Julia. Julia, their last surviving child, died during their stay in Beirut. The Lamartines spent three nights in this house in Plovdiv in 1833.

women are pretty with their long hair, mandatory blue jeans, and alluring necklines. Musicians and dancers perform streetside shows. In a park designed in the nineteenth century by a Swiss landscape architect,* there are crowds of athletes, lovers, and children. On an adjoining square, the country's political parties have set up tents and are making known their political platforms, for the country's legislative elections are only three days away. As far as we can tell, anti-communism is especially popular. People sitting outside cafes are passionately reinventing the world.

There's a strong sense of community life here. Elected representatives and residents are fiercely campaigning to have Plovdiv designated a European Capital of Culture in 2019.† Young Bulgarians volunteer to give English-language tours of the city. There's no charge, but tourists are invited to make a donation in support of other cultural projects. In the Old City, we stop near the statue of a violinist. He was famous during communism for having believed that he could get away with criticizing the regime. A few days later, he was arrested and was never heard from again. His friends raised money and erected this memorial statue. As darkness falls on this Indian-summer evening, girls and boys climb to the top of a high hill and gaze in contemplation of their three-thousand-year-old city, all aglow.

Some thirty years ago, the city decided to dig an underground walkway at a permanently congested intersection. No sooner had the backhoe begun to dig, than some fabulous ancient decorations appeared. The backhoes pulled out, and the archaeologists moved in. They uncovered a magnificent Roman house, with, as its centerpiece, the mosaic portrait of a woman—Irene—depicted in her home. The decision was then made to build the Museum Trakart at the

---

* TN: Ollivier is referring to Tsar Simeon's Garden, designed in 1892 by Lucien Chevalas (1840–1921), who was made an honorary citizen of Plovdiv and is sometimes called the "Minister of Flowers" for having created this park.
† TN: An honor Plovdiv would indeed receive.

site, directly beneath the intersection.* The cars would be rerouted. Irene's home dates from the second century, when Plovdiv was called Philippopolis, "Phillip's city," for King Phillip II of Macedon, Alexander the Great's father. The museum also contains a unique collection of some remarkable small translucent glass objects, representing the earth, the sky, wisdom, fire, and the points of the compass. They date from the fourth or fifth century and were discovered in tombs, either in Greece or in Bulgaria.

Bénédicte has acquired a taste for travel writing. It thrills me to see her every now and then in silent concentration. My guess is that she's busy cooking up a new journal entry, which our friends, upon our return, will tell us was a joy to read.

They, of course, couldn't count on me, the writer, to send postcards!

---

* TN: The Trakart Cultural Center opened May 24, 2004.

* * *

Harmanli, Bulgaria—October 5

The large fold in the Balkans that we've been following starting in Croatia begins to lose its ups and downs around Plovdiv, then flattens out all the way to the Black Sea, which finally swallows it up.

As a result, the road becomes a long, perfectly straight and flat ribbon, which also happens to be the main Sofia-Istanbul thruway, at least until the highway takes over for it.

In other words, we're no longer all alone on this cursed Republic Road I-8.

Two days with engines in my ears nonstop and no shoulder for an occasional breather has me feeling like I'm underwater and can't come up for air.

And when we discover that the hotel we tracked down at the last minute in Haskovo has a nightclub on the ground floor, and that it's Saturday night, I lose it.

Bernard, who typically has an uncanny ability to block out noise, couldn't take it anymore either. So we decided to give smaller roads a try, even if that would mean traveling extra miles and getting lost. Which would have happened if we hadn't come across a shepherd here, or a truck there. For it's always straight ahead until we come to a fork in the road. In which case, if there are no sheep in sight, it's heads or tails.

We won't be doing it again. Too many unknowns. Bucolic settings come at too great a cost. But we're incredibly happy to have headed out into the sunshine and filled up on silence and Bulgarian countryside, though it's not always the most cheerful place given the look of its dilapidated ghost towns, where, though we searched long and hard, we failed to find a single soul to guide us.

Along the roads, you find everything. Thousands of plastic bottles, all kinds of packaging, and, of course, cans—nice going, Red Bull!—umbrellas, pants, gunshot cartridges, earrings, hundreds of bolts (enough to open a hardware), pieces of automobiles, cat carcasses, dogs, foxes, snakes, hedgehogs, birds, fieldmice, weasels, and time and time again, ever since Italy, mini-altars in memory of road traffic accident victims.

In Bulgaria, they're more sophisticated than elsewhere. There's the mini-Orthodox church complete with dome; the mini-tomb made of marble or a simple stone slab, depending on the family's means; the photo of the deceased tacked to the fatal tree, sometimes with an incidental object, such as the fender of the red BMW in which one very young man killed himself. The victim and his assassin.

These are the only dead people we come across, those out-in-the-mid-dle-of-nowhere cemeteries having disappeared. But that's enough: we have no need to see any more.

Thankfully, more often, the beings we encounter are very much alive. Those selling grapes by the crateful to be used for making that famous alcohol, rakiya, or the tons of gourds that seem to appear out of nowhere. And the numerous Roma here, who throw us funny, curious gestures as they jolt along in their horse-drawn carts, or astride twenty-fifth-hand mopeds. In which case, the race is on! But come a downhill section, we lose every time.

When they're on foot, always with some indescribable rolling hand-cart, they immediately come to a halt in front of Ulysses, very intrigued. We try shooting the breeze, but for lack of a common language, never get very far.

Before heading off, they always hit us up for a few coins. On foot or on wheels, we're still non-Roma who, when evening rolls around, will sleep in (more or less) clean sheets, and never leave the dinner table hungry.

Starting in Croatia, we've come across two kinds of hotel:

A. The "That Ain't Working" Hotels,

B. The "That Works!" Hotels.

Category A includes two sub-categories:

A1. The "That Might Have Worked" Hotels,

A2. The "That Will Never Work" Hotels.

Subcategory A1 includes Soviet-style hotels, with 250 rooms and a 5,000-square-foot dining room for two guests. Three of our room's six lightbulbs "ain't working." There's a major leak in the bathroom. When the toilet refuses to flush, they put you in another room and lock the door to the first. The place has a squalid, refrigerated feel to it.

In subcategory A2, you have the nasty motels, from Room No 9 to 99. EVERYTHING in the bathroom leaks, including the loo, which hasn't seen a toilet brush since the day Tito died. The three lightbulbs, which date from the Cold War era, "aren't working." A wobbly fluorescent has been tacked up as a temporary fix. Anything you touch remains in your hand. The mattress is a couch frame, and, rather than sheep, you count the springs you're stretched out on, well into the wee hours of the morning. It's hovelesque.

Category B also includes two sub-categories:

B1. The "It More or Less Works" Hotels,

B2. The "It Works!" Hotels.

In sub-category B1, the leak in the bathroom is barely noticeable. The toilet seat drops down onto your back if you're a girl, and onto your you-know-what if you're a boy. Five out of six lightbulbs work.

In sub-category B2, all the bulbs work, NOTHING leaks (nothing that you notice, anyhow), there's a toaster at breakfast, a working computer in the hallway, and the place has a warm, friendly feel to it. And to top it all off, you don't get lost thanks to how clearly marked the directions to get there are. We've found only one of these: the Hotel Sonata in the city of Samokov, high up in the mountains. We'll give you their address any time you want.

We've also stayed with locals, in monasteries, in not-so-youthful youth hostels, in our tent, which has saved us more than once, and, most recently, in a chapel.

We're so tired each evening that we could sleep anywhere. And we're always thankful when we find a bed, a shower, and a sink in which we can wash our dirty clothes.

We find ourselves wondering whether we would be able to live full-time in these lands where everything is uncertain, and where people let time slip by, without running after it.

Bernard knows he couldn't keep himself from trying to fix everything that "isn't working," and me from trying to tidy up all the roadsides and all the garbage dumps all throughout the Balkans.

So much for that idea.

It isn't easy to change who you are.

The walker's body is indeed that amazing machine Bernard has been telling me about for a long time now. A little motor sitting at my sacrum propels me along, all by itself, and it runs on water. What a deal! But it took me a month to get it up and running.

The time I needed to learn slowness and patience.

Ulysses wore out his second pair of tires. We found new ones for him in Svilengrad, in a shop run by a fellow named Mitko.

We can get back underway.

So as to avoid Bulgaria's only road to Turkey, we're going to go on a two-day Greek holiday.

We've survived hordes of vacationers along the Adriatic, escaped landmines in Bosnia, Serbian serial killers, Kosovar thugs, and the snows of Bulgaria.

But will we survive all the noise???

You'll find out in the next episode!
BF

* * *

Plovdiv. October 1. We buckle up a small bag, leave our luggage with our landlady, and board the bus for Samokov, where we'll be attending a performance of the Grand National Folklore and Sound Ensemble of Bulgaria. We head back through Kostenets and Belovo, a curious village that's home to one of the country's largest paper mills. The inhabitants, eager to earn a little extra cash, buy huge quantities of toilet paper, then sell it retail to passing motorists. Some buildings' facades all but vanish behind a mountain of toilet paper rolls and paper towels.

Folk music is alive and well in Bulgaria, unlike in most European countries where it has vanished, swallowed up in the deluge of modern music. In the country's villages, this very unique musical form has been preserved. Several Bulgarian ensembles are invited each year to perform worldwide. Their polyphonies, both traditional and classical in nature, are sung by breathtakingly beautiful voices, which blend in atypical harmony. To our great surprise, the auditorium is three-quarters empty. We soon find out why: a Bulgarian soccer team is going head-to-head this evening with Real Madrid. Talk about unfair competition. But so much the better for Bénédicte, who chooses the best possible seats to record from. Seeing the joy on her face, I'm sure that she would have come all this way just for this evening's performance.

October 3. As we set out from Plovdiv, the air is freezing cold, and the forecast calls for afternoon rain. The only information we have is that there's no hotel in the town where we're planning to stop for the night. For our noon meal, we have soup and omelets in a grimy restaurant disguised as a fortified castle, and it costs us an arm and a leg. I express my surprise, but the waitress is surprised by my surprise. "You are," she tells me, "the only guests." Am I to understand that we have to pay a little extra so that she, her sister, and her husband—all three overweight—can eat? Well, if you put it that way . . . In a cafe a little farther along, the waitress promises us we'll find a hotel twenty kilometers (13 miles) down the road. Let's go then! We'd better get walking if we want to sleep somewhere dry.

A car pulls off the road with its hazard lights on. A man steps out, heads over to a tree, and gives it a big hug. Drawing near, I notice a photo tacked to the tree's trunk. That, in fact, is what he was hugging. A bouquet of flowers lies at the foot of the tree. We stop, and it's immediately clear that the man needs to talk. "Are you French? I traveled to your country, to Versailles, to visit my son when he was employed there for a French firm. His car plunged into the ditch, slammed into this tree, then came to a stop a short distance away in the field. My son had studied at the Sorbonne. He was first in his class. He was very talented and spoke several languages." The poster says that he was twenty-nine years old and that he died three months ago to the day. Next to the same tree are two engraved marble plaques. One is dedicated to the memory of a young man born in 1968, the second to a different boy, who died here in 2012. The father has a hard time controlling his emotions. His face appears to break out in what looks like goose bumps, he kisses the photo of his son a second time, then, without a word, he climbs back into his car and drives off toward Plovdiv, where he lives.

We walk among the dead here, and yet, though we're defenseless pedestrians, we sometimes have the strange feeling of being invulnerable.

Shortly afterward, in another car that passes us up, the man riding shotgun gives us an amicable wave. Two hundred yards farther, the car comes to a stop. The fellow gets out and grabs a bicycle secured to the roof. When we walk up to him, he asks us where we're from.

"From France."

"*De France? J'habite Paris. Je suis comédien.*"

"*Moi aussi,*" Bénédicte replies.

"*Je reviens du Festival d'Avignon.*"

"*Moi aussi.*"

*Quelle coïncidence!** The fellow, whose first name is Gherasim, left Paris on his bike in early September, bound for Svilengrad, his hometown.

"I'm traveling the same route—only in reverse—as the one I took when I was twenty years old to study with Marcel Marceau, the famous mime artist. Wherever I stop, I do a show. Last night, I performed in Plovdiv, and I'll be on stage again on October 9, in Svilengrad."

He hops back on his bike and rides off, followed by Nevena, his sister, the designated driver.

That morning, exasperated by thicker-than-ever traffic, we change course and head cross-country. A tiny road leads us to a village where, suddenly, we're the event of the day. But the group of fifteen or so young people who surround us isn't the least bit friendly. One of them asks if we belong to the mafia. French? At best, their faces reveal distrust, at worst, hostility. I start thinking to myself that we're in danger. The extreme poverty of this place, the potholed road running through the village, the hostile glares: it all looks like we've gotten ourselves into one doozy of a trap. My travels in Asia took me to places a lot like this, where all Europeans, no matter how broke, are thought to have the crown jewels of England stuffed away in their pockets. We run a very real risk of being attacked and robbed. So my guardian angel decides that something must be done.

A man in his forties pulls up in a car; he asks the young people a few questions, then, in perfect English, tells us point-blank: "Go back the way you came." Returning to the main highway is out of the question: it was to avoid the highway that we wound up here. The man scratches his head, then tells the young people smothering us to back off. He seems to hold sway over them, and only a half dozen or so refuse to comply; all the others walk away. So Lymbo—that's his name—asks us for a large piece of paper; on it, he draws the route

---

* TN: "From France? I live in Paris. I'm a stage actor." / "So am I," Bénédicte replies. / "I just returned from the Avignon Festival." / "So did I." / What a coincidence!

we need to take. But he warns us: there's neither road nor signpost, only dirt paths and very steep slopes. And, he adds, as if hoping to dissuade us even more, we'll be skirting a military zone, where live-fire exercises take place every day. He turns to the young people, asks them a question, then adds: "Today's Sunday, so maybe they won't be doing any shooting."

We take the blacktopped road he shows us: it soon turns into a gravel road with deep potholes, before becoming just a simple path through the hills. I turn around two or three times to be sure we're not being followed. With Ulysses in tow, who's jouncing from wheel to wheel, we're sweating buckets despite the chilly air. We finally reach the summit. The view is so breathtaking that we plop ourselves down in the grass and revel in all the wild beauty before us. The path splits in two, turns, disappears for a while, then reappears. We walk past a building downhill from the path. A soldier pops out of a sentry box and observes us through binoculars. In the little village of Momina, all but three or four houses are in ruins. What path should we take? Three or four different ones lead out of the village, but there are no signs. We've gotten ourselves in an awful mess. I knock at a door to make inquiries. A Romany family lives there, and—for a small fortune—the father immediately offers to drive me to Harmanli, our destination. His daughter, about twelve years old with bright green eyes, stretches a hand out toward me, sliding her thumb over her index finger. Once again, I can feel their eyes on me as if I were a pot of gold. Imitating what I've seen people do in Orthodox churches, I exit the house walking backwards; only in my case, it's so that I don't get pounced on. After a good many ups and downs, and a little wandering, punctuated by a handful of not-so-hostile encounters, we arrive—on our last legs—at the Hotel Ralitsa (the name means "larkspur"), a few miles from Harmanli. The extra distance of this Sunday hike was offset by sublime landscapes and silences. Still, we travel over twenty-four miles. Very unreasonable. And, all things considered, even with its speeding vehicles and deafening noise, the highway may well be less dangerous than the countryside.

At 7:00 in the morning, Harmanli is an absolutely dismal city. Ramshackle factories, shuttered hotels overrun by weeds, empty streets, and houses spiked with antennas and satellite dishes in the hope of pulling in as many TV stations as possible, the modern opium of the people. We order breakfast in a greasy spoon whose owner assures us that the price—indicated in lev, Bulgaria's currency—is the same in euros, making it twice as expensive. Given how modest the bill is, though, I couldn't care less, and, though he takes me for a perfect imbecile, I pretend to believe him.

We are, of course, on the Silk Road. In Bulgarian, the word is *svila*, and city or village is *grad*. Svilengrad and the surrounding area once produced great quantities of cocoons for export to France and Italy. In the nineteenth century, silkworm disease decimated the industry. But Svilengrad was lucky to be located on the main road to Turkey, and consequently was able to maintain its economic stability to some extent. We reach the city by way of a road which, a large billboard tells us, was built by the European Union for the modest sum of twelve million euros. And—in what is for us an all-too-rare delight—a highway was put in parallel to it. The road we're traveling is nearly deserted. At this stage of the game, we're relatively confident of our fitness, since we've been covering between twenty-two and twenty-five miles per day without our aches, though still present, ever becoming overly painful.

As we're crossing Svilengrad's main square, hotel-hunting as usual at the end of the day, a window slides open in the facade of what appears to be a municipal building. Out pops a head: it's Gherasim. He arrived here several days ago on his bike. He's helping a group of young people get ready for a show. His mother invites us to dinner. Slava Dichlieva is a delightful woman who speaks perfect French. Which should come as no surprise since she's been teaching our native tongue all her life. And it's no doubt because he was weaned on French culture that her son decided to emigrate to our home-land. We dine in her yard undeterred by the cool autumn air, beside a large wood fire. Slava spends part of the year in Svilengrad and the remainder in Sofia, the country's capital. She cooked up some delicious meatballs for us, and a side of cheese-stuffed red peppers, drizzled in a delicious sauce. What a treat! Slava's thrilled to be able to use her French. We ask about Bulgaria's legislative elections, which just took place. The Turkish minority, which had run a very active campaign despite representing only a small minority, did quite well, garnering 14 percent of the vote; the Christians, on the other hand, who ran a disorganized campaign, spread across some twenty tickets, find themselves destabilized, and the country, our hostess tells us, is wondering how, with such fragmentation, it will ever be possible to form a government. We also talk some about literature. After shamelessly mentioning that I recently published my first novel, *Histoire de Rosa qui tint le monde dans sa main** (The Story of Rosa Who Held the World in Her Hand), I promise to send Slava a copy upon our return home. After finally reading it, she'll send me a thank-you note saying what a rare privilege it was to have an author send her a book—and a French author at that!

Early the next morning, Gherasim picks us up at the hotel and drives us to the home of Mitko Petrov, who coaches the cycling team he rides with. Mitko offers us new tires to replace Ulysses's old ones, which look ready to burst. Mitko swaps them out while we go for coffee. Upon our return, he timidly hands me the bill: sixteen levs (about $9). To make up for what, in his eyes, is a hefty price, he throws in a spare inner tube for free.

It's past noon by the time we cross the marvelous, sixteen-arched Mustafa-Pacha Bridge over the Maritsa River. It's one of the earliest designs by Mimar Sinan, Turkey's most famous architect, who was to revolutionize the art of mosque-building. Edirne, the first Turkish city beyond the border, is seventeen miles away via a very busy highway, which, for us, would surely be a motor-filled nightmare. No way are we going to take it. To spare our nerves, our ears, and to avoid getting killed, we opt instead for a grand thirty-four-mile detour

---

* Paris: Éditions Phébus, 2013.

through Greece. After going through customs, we find ourselves on another splendid road: a four-lane highway, financed once again by Europe, but completely deserted. A few miles away, just over the border, we spot the more direct Svilengrad-Edirne Highway we so dreaded, and, on it, hundreds of cars and trucks zip back and forth. Our euphoria at having this brand-new, deserted road, is, however, short-lived, for we soon realize that we are, in fact, this ultra-secure throughway's prisoners: high metal barriers designed to keep animals from venturing out onto the pavement also prevent pedestrians from making side trips into neighboring villages. The miles tick by, and before long, we're thirsty. We've gone through all our water and need to find more. Around 5:00 p.m., we finally come to an off ramp, and ask some workmen inside a building-materials storage enclosure for water.

The zone, planted with cotton, is marshy, and as soon as the temperature drops, mosquitoes—which I hate—mount an attack. Though I'm slathered with repellent, the nasty bugs always some-how find those few square millimeters of unprotected skin, which their stingers find so tasty. We begin a desperate search for shelter. There's no point dreaming of a hotel, the workmen left us with no hope of that. Down a small parallel road, a miracle: a totally isolated Orthodox chapel, and the door's unlocked. Out front is a small, flow-er-filled square with a water faucet. We park Ulysses around back, then settle in. The building is small and consists of two sections. A kind of common room of a few square yards with some chairs and, on a table, a board game. The other section is markedly more religious, with icon and candles. When two women arrive on foot from Dikaia, the next village over, we fear they'll kick us out. Not at all: they come here each evening to lock the door for the night. After we've told them why we're here, they talk it over, and the one convinces the other to let us spend the night. Then off they go, all smiles, after wishing us a pleasant night in the light of the church candles they lit.

In the morning, as we're preparing to leave, a van stops, and a man gets out to wash his hands at the courtyard spigot. Bénédicte greets him in Bulgarian, since she has no idea how to say it in Greek. He returns to his vehicle and comes back with a loaf of bread and two raisin cakes, which he offers her. He explains that he's Bulgarian, and that he comes to Greece to sell his bread. Slack-jawed at this unexpected, spontaneous gift, before Bénédicte can even say "thank you," the van drives off.

XIX

ADRIANOPLE—EDIRNE

Turkey (Türkiye). Population: 79.4 million. A secular country at the wish of Atatürk, the father of the nation. A large majority of the population is Muslim. The Kurdish minority is represented by the PKK, the Kurdistan Workers' Party, whose leader, Öcalan, is serving life in prison. Negotiations for membership in the European Union began . . . over twenty-seven years ago (1987). Currency: the Turkish lira. Capital city: Ankara. Largest city: Istanbul.

I had somewhat forgotten that Greece and Turkey get along about as well as two dogs and one bone. For the first time since setting out from Lyon, we find armed soldiers at the border crossing, with assault rifles over their shoulders. We've made a practice of snapping a selfie in front of each country's welcome sign. Today, October 8, 2014, we cross our eleventh border and, just as we're about to perform that ritual out in front of the Turkish customs office, a soldier, waving his weapon, authoritatively discourages us. A placard confirms the gesture: NO PHOTOS. We take our first few steps in Turkey feeling a little frustrated, but then find, far from any police officers, a signpost that proclaims "*TÜRKIYE*," which fits the bill perfectly. In the first village, seated outside a teahouse, three little old men are chatting away. The moment they see us, they motion us over: "*Gel! Chai!*" (Come! Tea!). Cheerful fellows with infectious laughs, all together the three have no more than ten teeth. Without the slightest hesitation, they exchange virile handshakes with Bénédicte. In a flash, the teahouse's owner arrives with his little tulip cups filled to the brim. They're shaped like Calvados snifters, or *demoiselles*: slender in the middle, slightly flared at the top, and quite small.* The Turks knock them back from morning to night. The men beg us to tell them our story. And when we leave, everyone's thrilled by this first encounter, them as much as us. Now we're off to Edirne.

Just as Byzantium was transformed into Constantinople before becoming Istanbul, Edirne was once Adrianople,† and was even the capital of the Ottoman Empire from the mid-fourteenth to the mid-fifteenth century. The city was buffeted by the winds of history. In May 1913, it was no longer Turkish but Bulgarian; then, three months later, it was Turkish again. In 1920, it was handed over to Greece and reassumed the name of Adrianople, only to be handed back to Turkey in 1923 and renamed yet again. It's a beautiful city of intertwined histories. Wikipedia tells me that, in the nineteenth century, the city's population included, among others, thirty thousand Muslims, twenty-two thousand Greeks, and twelve thousand Jews. Edirne is traversed by the Maritsa River, which we saw first in Plovdiv, then in Svilengrad. At the heart of the city is the *Saraçlar Cadde* (*sa-ra-chlar djah-deh,* Saddlers Street), a wide, pedestrian-only boulevard, ablaze with the oriental colors of fabrics, fruit, and fish. Customers turn back the fishes' bright red gills to be certain of their freshness. Right next door, three young men busily grill the fish the customers purchase, who then consume them on tables lined up on the sidewalk. Here, street vendors are king. Those who lack a brick-and-mortar shop sell their merchandise straight from a cart; those who haven't a cart carry their wares in rectangular baskets suspended from their necks or perched atop their heads. The friendly, protective feel of the *Rüstempaşa Kervansarayı*—the Rüstem-Pacha Caravansary—plunges me right back into the world of the Silk Road and those "Camel Palaces," where business is conducted with feigned

---

* TN: *Demoiselles* typically hold ten centiliters (just shy of four liquid ounces).
† TN: In Latin, it's Hadrianopolis, after the famous Roman emperor.

nonchalance while sipping cups of tea that never go empty. Everything can be haggled over; merchants and customers sit on pouffes or stools in cell-like rooms, each with a surface area of about two square yards. Turkish business culture always involves abundance. Vegetable sacks overflow, jewelry store windows shimmer with gold, and in pastry shops, honey cakes softly glisten. Vendors spot us from afar, and in our case, the tourist rate applies. The price is never displayed anyway, for negotiation must always be preserved. It's both the spice and the driver of trade in the Orient.

We walk past two young girls in school uniforms. For, in Turkey, a secular country, the egalitarian uniform is required, and head coverings forbidden, at least in school. But we also notice a young woman in shorts moving through the crowd, magnetizing the glowing gazes of all the men in the pedestrian boulevard to the small of her back. Noise is part and parcel of everyday life here. Though conversation is discreet in stores and cafes, out in the street, young people noisily shout to one another. The girls, all in European dress, mix right in with the boys, and they horse around as one big group. Our thoughts go to the women and girls of Kosovo, whom we practically never saw. In Edirne, we find ourselves between two eras and two universes. A computer store stands right next door to one of those tiny spice shops, talced with powders exhaling oriental fragrances.

Out in front of the Selimiye Mosque, we find a garden, benches, silence. We immerse ourselves in a bubble of serenity. Like the Mustafa-Pacha Bridge, this UNESCO World Heritage Site is the work of Sinan, the most famous Turkish architect of all time.* Its four minarets are the tallest in all the Muslim world. Its interior is vast, its lines pure, the light unreal. We lose ourselves in blissful admiration. As the sun begins to sink in the west, the light pouring in from the dome is simply magical. A child noisily plays about; visitors snap pictures; old men, back from the market with shopping bags at their feet, jabber away. Footsteps are muffled by long-pile

---

* TN: Mimar Sinan (about 1490 to July 17, 1588).

wool carpets. A mosque is, of course, a place of prayer, but it's a place of life too, quite unlike the stuffy atmosphere and stony inflexibility of our churches back home, almost exclusively devoted to religious services.

I walk up and down the little streets in search of a cobbler, for the heel of one of my boots, already patched up in Plovdiv, is threatening to come loose again. It has only about 150 miles or so of pavement pounding left to go. With a little luck, it will last to the end.

* * *

Lüleburgaz, Turkey—October 13

Dropping in on the Greeks was a smart move. We came to an empty highway, abandoned by all the cars and trucks crammed bumper-to-bumper a few miles to the north, on the Bulgarian side.

We cut across this little corner of Greece on our deserted road like pashas, rolling down the emergency lane and taking our time. Until we ran out of water, that is.

When that happens, you're keener on finding the next exit than when, in a car, you miss the one you meant to take.

The little white balls of cotton, clinging to the hillsides like so many clumps of snow, had us fooled for a few miles; they kept us distracted until we were finally able to refill our water bags.

One last souvenir of Orthodox Europe: as we were leaving the chapel where we spent the night, a Bulgarian baker, stopping to drink water at the fountain, offered us a loaf of bread and two little raisin cakes, just like that, without us even having told him our story. A gift. Did he take us for something we were not? Who knows? In any event, thank you, Bulgarian Baker! We won't soon forget the taste of your bread.

Arriving in Turkey was incredibly exotic! First, because we were welcomed at customs by soldiers gripping assault rifles (goodbye twenty-eight member states of the European Union!), but especially by three old-timers in a cafe who wanted us to join them for çay (chai: the real deal, straight from a samovar!) in the first village before Edirne, the largest city after the border.*

We're delighted to have minarets back again, which had vanished in Bulgaria, but above all that same joyful, child-like spontaneity we

---

* TN: That number today is twenty-seven, after the United Kingdom's exit from the European Union on January 31, 2020.

came across in Kosovo. Everyone's outside, and we're greeted with cheery cries of "Merhaba!" (Hello!). Kids come running for a closer look at our gear; the honks of cars, trucks, tractors, and mopeds are all friendly and backed up by broad smiles.

This time, we are really here. This is the Orient.

Edirne, which we feared would be inaccessible and ugly like so many other large cities, lets you draw serenely near, along the banks of a river that might as well be the Loire. Charming and indolent, the city is packed with mosques, the largest of which is stunningly beautiful. It leaves us speechless.

This is a welcome day off for I need to dry out a little blister that's appeared on my left heel, who knows why. A highway effect no doubt: I got carried away by how fast we could go.

Another pleasant surprise: Route D100, which we'll be following all the way to Istanbul, looks just like its Greek counterpart. A kind of half-deserted highway, with a paved shoulder nearly six feet wide—and it's all ours! A luxury worthy of Byzantium . . . or rather, Constantinople. Or rather . . . well, you know what I mean!

We set out beneath a sun as radiant as our morale, through countryside where spinning, turning, sputtering tractors perform an autumnal ballet in preparation for the coming planting season. And to complete their job of ravaging the land.

We still have a long way to go before intensive farming is a thing of the past.

We're happy as clams on our asphalt strip where danger is no longer on our heels, and we can walk side by side. We're able to return to our conversations, our "worst-pun" games, and our blessed silences.

I'm still learning my lines for the play I'm going to be in. I'm going to have to work on it even more when I get home, since memorization takes focus, and, in the end, that requires peace and quiet. We stop to drink a cup of çay at the next gas station, then get back underway, singing at *the top of our lungs:* "Tant mieux si la route est longue, nous ferons le tour du monde!"*

With the sun and our shorter stages, the blissful days of siestas are back again, which we so sorely missed. They're moments of pure joy, during which the mind, finally quelled by fatigue, gratefully capitulates. Sleep like that is worth its weight in gold.

My preference goes to public benches or the stone steps of a stairway. In the grass, you're inevitably eaten alive by a colony of ants or some other creepy-crawlies that decide to clamber up your legs starting with your toes' north face.

Too many critters live in the grass.

In a field, the alternative is a tarp, from which you can see the enemy approaching from afar.

T-minus five. The countdown has begun.

Will we get there ahead of the rain? You'll find out you-know-when!

BF

---

* TN: "Who cares if the road is long? We'll travel round the world!" From "Le tour du monde" ("The Journey Round the World"), a 1955 hit song by Jean-Claude Darnal (1929–2011).

XX

DRAWING NEAR

Setting out from the beautiful city of Edirne, we have ten stages left to go. The prospect plunges me into a melancholic meditation. The end of the road will soon be here. There's every indication that we'll make it to the finish line and enter Istanbul hand in hand. Starting in Lyon, our boots have trod the soil of twelve different countries.* Back when we were still in the Capital of Roman Gaul—as that city is sometimes called—success seemed beyond our grasp, and I feared we wouldn't physically hold up, but today, we're seasoned walkers. I can now glimpse the end of this marvelous and adventurous interlude in our busy lives. When personal reflection is counterbalanced by the mundane management of day-to-day life, whether the charting of our course, or the never-ending quest for food and a bed. There's nothing more stimulating than going anywhere you want with an eye to figuring out where you're from, and where you want to go. This retreat from our ordinary lives, this casting-off of mooring lines, has reset our life counters to zero. The ever-changing cities, cultures, languages, faces, and landscapes; that extra effort required when, at the end of the day, the muscles suddenly give out and the foot slips—all that will, in a few days, be coming to an end.

But even so, I have no regrets. Other images come to my mind: of the house, of the wood I need to chop for the winter, of pleasant

---

* TN: France, Italy, Slovenia, Croatia, Bosnia and Herzegovina, Montenegro, Serbia, Kosovo, North Macedonia, Bulgaria, Greece, and Turkey.

evenings by the fireside, and of friends dropping by. At the end of this journey, I navigate between two pleasures, between two very different worlds: one governed by the chimes of my hundred-year-old grandfather clock, the other by the muezzin's call to prayer. I don't want to give up this one for that. Before long, though, we're going to have to detach from all this detachment and go back to international news, the counting of victims, and that tsunami of demoralizing commercials. A journey like this one will make you a dedicated supporter of Degrowth.* We rediscovered, for a few weeks, the values of that far-off world in which belief is more precious than life, and no one is obsessed by objects. Life is about to catch back up with us, set our heads spinning, and trick us onto paths that are not necessarily any less dangerous than those we've been traveling since we set out from Lyon.

From here to Istanbul, the road is straight as an arrow and not very congested thanks to a parallel highway. We'll walk anywhere from fifteen to nineteen miles a day, a virtual Sunday stroll. On the road to Havsa, our first stop, villages sit back some distance, away from the noise. We drop into service stations where, at the entrance, there's always a samovar ready to spit out free tea—and you don't even have to buy gas. "Yes, yes! Free!" insists a delightful young woman, who can't help but smile at the disbelief of these two strangers from a world where everything comes at a cost. At midday, picnic and siesta in the grass for the first time in ages.

Havsa is a lifeless city. Closed shops, with grass growing in front of some doorsteps. The main thoroughfare is full of craters, as if road repairs had been interrupted after the old asphalt had been broken up. Cars crawl along, trying to avoid the potholes while stirring up clouds of dust that eventually settle down over the houses, patios, and people. The *pansiyon* where we sleep beats all previous records in

---

* TN: The Degrowth Movement (*la Décroissance*), which points out that endless economic growth on a finite planet is impossible, is, considering the climate crisis, a hot topic in contemporary French politics.

terms of dreariness, dry faucets, and filth. Between the building it's in and the next, a large, putrid pit serves as the public dump. In each *çay salonu* (tearoom), the owner imagines he's swindling us by charging seven euros ($8.50) for two omelets, two honey desserts, and four mugs of tea. Later, on the road, a cyclist comes to a stop and hands us two candy bars—"Take it! Take it!"—then pedals off. The chocolate tastes of the joy of our exchange, of unpretentious humanity.

Farther along, we come across a truck driver having a bite to eat:

"*Araban varmı?*" (Do you have a car?)

"*Arabam yok.*" (No.)

He can't believe his ears. He hands us a bottle of water and two packages of chocolate cookies. We were almost dry, Bénédicte having lost her canteen, and what was left in mine wasn't enough for two. Offering to pay for his gifts would have been a serious insult, in total disregard of this country's hospitable culture.

In Babaeski, where the road is just as torn up as in Havsa, a sprinkler runs nonstop. The upside: we breathe less dust. The downside: we have to tramp through mud beneath a burning sun. In front of the mosque, forty-some men stand facing the imam. Slightly back of them, seated on benches, are a dozen women, all wearing headscarves. There's a coffin on trestles. The imam, dressed all in white, utters a short eulogy for the deceased, who died overnight. The men then move aside, the coffin is loaded into a white van, and two men climb in next to it. The imam takes the "death seat" up front, and then everyone heads off to the cemetery. In the Muslim faith, the dead must be buried less than twenty-four hours after they've drawn their last breath.

Today, October 12, shortly before noon, a long-distance cyclist—a woman who is visibly European—passes us up, then does a U-turn (the road is deserted at this hour), then comes toward us. Dunya is from the German-speaking part of Switzerland, and she set out from Davos, where she lives, on the very same day that we boarded the train to Verona. Tomorrow afternoon, she'll be in Istanbul where she plans on spending two weeks before taking off again for Iran, and then India, along with her father. She snaps a photograph of us as we're walking along with Ulysses, which is something that, till now, no one else had done: it will be the only photo of the journey in which the two of us appear.

A little later, as we're walking past a big, brand-new building, a cry of "*Gel! Çay!*" stops us in our tracks. Siliktas, the security guard for this nearly completed nursing home, worked for six months in Austria. But when he wanted to return there, he couldn't get a visa. He tells us that in Gaza this summer, 2,200 people have been killed. The world's catastrophes are already catching up to us. My two feet are increasingly painful. It's time we reach our destination. Leaving Lüleburgaz the next morning, we hear a voice calling out to us. It's Dunya, who also slept in this city, and is now on her way to Istanbul.

That evening, in our hotel's lobby—dominated by an immense portrait of Atatürk, omnipresent in this country—a noisy group of friends in the reception area sets about asking us questions. One fellow wants to know my age. Not knowing how to say it in Turkish, I jot it down: 75. The flatterer switches the digits around and tells me that I could pass for 57. In our room, the hotel's owners wanted to save money by installing a motion detector for the light fixture in the bathroom. But they adjusted the timer to switch off too soon, after about thirty seconds. So, to brush your teeth, you have to hold your toothbrush in one hand and wave the other to get the light back on. Sitting on the toilet is a hoot: we have to wave our hands as if we were saying goodbye. As for the shower, the detector doesn't reach that far, which forces us to wash up in total darkness.

At Büyük, the hotel we reach late the next afternoon proudly proclaims on a plaque that it's the regular meeting place for members of the Lion's and Rotary clubs. One detail is missing, though, as we'll soon discover. As we're getting ready for bed, booming music echoes through the building. Two overly made-up and perfumed women, who are none other than the establishment's own shills, tell me that there's a nightclub on the ground floor, and that the party won't stop until 6:00 in the morning. Furious, I get dressed and storm down to the reception desk. While I'm speaking with the receptionist, a portly fellow walks up wearing a silk tie, endless French cuffs, and gold rings on all his fingers. He introduces himself: he's the owner. In English, I throw an epic tantrum: "You ought to warn people that you rent out rooms where no one could ever sleep! I'm giving you a choice: either you turn down the music, or you refund me what I paid up front for the room." I of course expect the fellow to send me packing. Cheats never give you back your money. He appears to hesitate. I lay it on thick. He plays the stingy card, offering to refund me 50 percent of what I paid. Half a night, if you will. "Nothing doing: I don't half sleep, so either reimburse me in full, or pull the plug on the music." He finally gives in, and the receptionist painfully takes the banknotes back out that he had rung up three hours earlier. And so here we are, out in the cold night air, in search of a bed. Nedim, the owner of the restaurant where we had eaten dinner, tells us about a nearby *pansiyon*; but then, on second thought, he closes his shop and takes us there himself. Unfortunately, there's not a single room left. So we wind up sleeping in Nedim's dining room, lullabied all night long by noisy refrigerator motors, which kick on each time we close our eyes. Having kindly offered to put us up, trusting and selfless, the owner hands us the key and requests only that we leave it on the door when we're ready to head back out.

XXI

BACK TO ISTANBUL

State Road D100's monotonous ribbon stretches off into the distance. We settle into a routine, the traffic grows heavier, rain has now begun to fall. The forecast promises terrible weather for the day we planned to arrive in Istanbul. So we'll stretch out the stages to get there a day earlier. In Çorlu (*chor'-lu)*, we ask two men enjoying drinks at a table outside a restaurant whether they know of a hotel. They get up, lead us to a comfortable inn, stick around long enough to make sure we're not charged the tourist rate, then bid us farewell, reassured. Such kind people! The next morning, as we're on our way out of town, a man who introduces himself as an elected city official stops us, asks a few questions, marvels at our story, then wants to buy us breakfast. We just had ours and it would take us too long to explain that I'm a U-turn-ophobe. We thank him and hurry off.

As we close in on Istanbul, the road becomes increasingly congested. It's difficult walking, for there's no side strip for pedestrians. Whenever we can, we veer off in the direction of a village, such as Akçaköy today, where we catch our breath the time it takes us to down a cup of çay beneath an arbor. Fruit vendors set up all along the road call out to us in friendly voices. Occasionally, one of them offers us tea. Yesterday, it was Dohum, who asked me my age: "*Mashallah!*"* Today, it's Nestrine, a brunette with large, light green eyes, as

---

* Meaning, "What a marvel God has created!" or, more simply, "Incredible!" (TN: cf. *Walking to Samarkand*, Chapter V).

193

luminous as if lit from within. Nestrine chuckles at our fascination with her irises, fringed with long lashes. Waves of friendship emanate from her eyes to ours and hold us back. But the road tugs harder still. We have to get back underway.

October 16. From our hotel window, we catch sight of the immense metropolis's flashing lights. After thirty miles on the road, we climb into bed, bone-tired. How very long those last steps of a long walk are, before the saving shower.

* * *

Çorlu, Turkey—October 14: T-Minus Four Days

I have a new subcategory to add to category A, the "That Ain't Working" hotels.

It's category A3: The "Don't Push the Customer" hotels.

They have every feature of subcategory A2, the "That Will Never Work" hotels, along with a few extras, namely, the lack of a bedspread (which is probably just as well), an exorbitant rate for such a nasty place, and the surprise of the evening: a nightclub in the hotel basement! When the bass notes started booming around 8:30 p.m., it reminded us of that awful Bulgarian nightclub/hotel, and we immediately lost our cool.

Bernard, grandiose as ever in sticky situations like this, went straight to see the two lazybones at the reception desk and gave them the choice of either turning the music way down or, barring that, giving us our money back on the spot. I should point out that we did have a Plan B, which is why we were able to raise such a stink (an extremely rare situation when you're traveling on foot!): a pansiyon *that Nedim, a local restaurant owner, had recommended.*

The men try negotiating a half-price deal; Bernard retorts that we have no intention of sleeping for only half a night. The owner, pimp-like with his rings and shiny shoes, eventually hands us back our dough—it ain't easy arguing with an irate Bernard! We pack our bags lickety-split, then off we go, our gear on our backs, slamming the door on this brothel and dragging our cart across the once-red carpet.

Outside, we pray that we didn't just trade substance for shadows. It's 10:00 p.m. and it's cold out. We dash over to Nedim's to let him know the good news and he shows us the way to the pansiyon.

No vacancy. Gulp!

Our last resort: sleeping in Nedim's restaurant. With countless gestures, including the pantomime of an inflatable mattress, we explain our latest request. Here's hoping he says yes, otherwise it's tent-in-the-park and cops-in-the-night.

*"Tamam" (okay), he says, shaking his head from left to right, which, though somewhat disconcerting for West Europeans, confirms what he said. Bulgarians do the same thing: nodding up and down means "no" (*ne*) and shaking your head from side-to-side means "yes" (*da*). A real headache, let me tell you.*

In a nutshell, though we nearly gave ourselves stiff necks, we grasped that we'd be sleeping with a roof over our heads. Whew! And who cares if the refrigerated display case kicked on at regular intervals all through the night, sounding like a washing machine on spin? It was still better than the subwoofers back at the nightclub!

The following morning, not quite awake, we head back out with the sun coming up over Highway D100, which is less and less deserted. Istanbul is now only eighty-one miles away: the situation is going to get worse, that's for sure.

In lieu of breakfast, we finish off a package of cookies a truckdriver gave us yesterday when we asked him for water.

Now we need a cup of çay. For that, we carefully choose our gas stations. At PO (Petrol Ofisi) and OPET (Öztürkler Petrol), çay is offered for free; elsewhere, foreigners like us get swindled out of a lira or two. But enough already, we won't be falling for that!

This morning, our server's name is Zeki, and he's tickled pink to pose with Ulysses. As for us, we're incredibly happy to encounter in this slice of life people so genuinely, so plainly nice. After two cups of çay and a photo, we offer one another a kiss on the cheek as if we'd known each other our entire lives, then off we go.

What a joy life can sometimes be to live!

Between two cups of çay—pffffitt!—a tire bursts. This latest pair lasted just seven days. We're going to have to speak to Metko about this. . . . We saw it coming, though, and had picked up a right-sized spare in Havsa. We'll need yet another before we're done—to Bernard's great dismay—for he never likes to replace a tire until it bursts! No, but honestly.

After agriculture, now industry is becoming intensive, with huge textile and chemical factories spewing countless gallons of oily, fuming, purple liquid into the local river. It's terrifying.

The noise is back, but it won't be the death of us!

BF

* * *

Ihlan waits for customers beside the road and, laughing, watches our strange caravan draw near. Behind him is a small van full of cages into which he has placed his birds for sale. There's a scale on the vehicle's tailboard, for he sells his poultry by weight. Our arrival draws him from his boredom. Learning that we're going to Istanbul, he alerts us: at the spot we happen to be, we're heading directly for the highway. Allah preserve us! You have to go *that* way, he tells us. And he points to a road a hundred yards away that will lead us to the adjacent village of Selimpaşa, where we'll find the road we want. The problem is that, between that road and us, there are two hellishly busy lanes of highway traffic, and high guardrails on either side. We get right down to business. Ihlan, who's built like a slightly potbellied colossus, abandons his fine feathered friends and grabs Ulysses; working together, the three of us lift our cart over a first guardrail; we then run between two groups of cars, clear another guardrail, another roadway, sprint a third time, clamber over a final guardrail, and *voilà*, we're back on the right road. Thrilled, Ihlan waves us goodbye, then goes back to his chickens, slaloming his way between the roaring, lethal cars.

After a tasty çorba (*chor'-ba*)—the Turks make marvelous soups—the Sea of Marmara, shining off in the distance, catches our eyes as we round a bend on a gentle downhill stretch. Why not go dip our toes in it? A few buildings separate the road from the beach. Near a pier, three women are busily chatting away beside two large tables on which an ocher-colored powder has been spread out to dry. We're not certain what it consists of, though it seems to be for making çorba throughout the winter, which is already in the air. Waves are softly breaking over the beach. With Ulysses beside me, I sit for a moment on the pier to savor that sweet-and-salty dish known as "the end of a long walk." Bénédicte has started up a long discussion with one of the women. With the sea for a backdrop, having trouble understanding one another yet getting along so well has them laughing. On the road, two children are playing with a wooden crate they've put wheels on. Their dream is to own a car; ours is to walk. They watch us go by, indifferent to all that is not their wagon.

* * *

Istanbul!—October 17

You're gonna laugh: we missed the sign indicating that we'd reached the city! So no selfie.

Too many traffic lanes, too many cars, too many guardrails, too many medians, too much of everything: Istanbul is one gigantic megacity stretching for thirty miles!

We're happy, very happy to have made it here.

BF

* * *

Arriving in a megalopolis such as Istanbul is like climbing to the top of a mountain pass. At each bend, you think you see the summit, but it's always farther away. To be honest, the city's so big that we never exactly know where we are. The last few miles are a real obstacle course: two high hills to scale, nonexistent or broken-up sidewalks, an endless crowd, traffic from hell.

Having decided, go figure, that we have no desire to be mown down right at the finish line, we call it a day on a beach beside a parking garage, thirteen miles from the center of the city. I take our tool kit out and start disassembling Ulysses, piece by piece: he goes back into his duffel bag. And that's where he'll remain until we're home. We hop on a bus, and it lets us off at Taksim Square, the heart of Istanbul. On this vast square, just a few days ago, government security forces clashed with Turkish Kurds. The Kurds were pressuring Erdoğan's government to allow their armed brothers in the Afrin District and the city of Qamishli to provide military assistance to Syrian Kurds, who, for several weeks, had been resisting attacks from the Islamic State in the border city of Kobanî. The regime eventually allowed the relief column to pass, and Kobanî was liberated.

In the bus, I observe Bénédicte with fondness and admiration. How marvelous this woman of mine is. I've watched her limp along, gritting her teeth to make it just a little farther, and, with a heavy heart, even agreeing to two mandatory rest periods, for we faced a real risk of having to throw in the towel. But it was in the day-to-day that she moved me most. My little "bourgeoise"—who loves slowly waking up in the morning—revealed a penchant for adventure. Though a real food lover, she put up with having to skip meals. She never once complained when, in the morning, though reeking of diesel fumes, we had to slip back into the previous day's dirt, for lack of a bathroom or even a simple spigot. But it's in the way she relates to others that she made me fall even more deeply in love with her than at the start of our journey. Bénédicte is a bright light, an eternal flame. At each encounter, people turned to her and opened their hearts. Her ready ear turned the tongue-tied into chatterboxes. And that suited me perfectly well since, given my bad memory, which can hold no more than ten words in each new language, I was then able to simply stand back and observe this open-minded, astute woman, who never once lost her sense of humor—even when people mistook her for my daughter! *Minerale, naturale*—Bénédicte has proven herself both strong and resolute from one end of this journey to the other.

Our friend Jérôme Bastion, correspondent for Radio France in Turkey, who welcomed us into his home, has been on the go these past several days updating European news outlets on the recent clashes between Jihadists and Kurdish combatants. Lovely Güler, his partner, is a newscaster for the Kurdish television channel. As we dine on the waterfront—once all the outpourings are over—they apprise us of what's going on not just in the Middle East, but in Europe as well. We soon have our fill of tragedies, power struggles, and crises, both social and economic. During our brief stay in the beautiful city of Istanbul, where history crops up at every turn, we also have lunch with our piquant friend Aslıhan, in a charming restaurant overlooking the Bosporus this time. Farewell, holidays! The adventure is almost over.

At the airport, I mutter aloud that I need a third Turkish lira coin so I can use one of the luggage trolleys available to travelers. I can only find two. A man spins around and places the coin I'm missing into my hand, then dashes off before I can say *Teşekkür ederim* (Thank you so much).

In the airplane, I start thinking things over and try to quell the nostalgia that holds sway each time a long walk comes to an end. Yes, I am happy to have followed through with Bénédicte's suggestion; to have triumphed over my fears and weaknesses; to have come face to face with so many lives, so many cultures, so many landscapes, and all this immense history; and to have finally traveled the entire Silk Road, all 9,300 miles (15,000 km) of it.

Fifteen years ago, I somewhat naively set out on a 7,500-mile (12,000 km) walk, seriously doubting my ability to make it all the way to distant Xi'an, with four deserts to cross and the fearsome Pamirs in my way. I set out from the city of Lyon with the exact same doubts. And here we are at the finish line. We evidently possess inner resources we didn't know we had.

I smile, thinking of the question I'll surely soon be asked: *And so, what about your next trip?*

Kindly let me process this one first.

* * *

Back Home—October 24

It took a little over three hours for the plane carrying us back to Paris to go the eighteen hundred miles (3,000 km) we needed four months to walk.

 So why do the journey on foot?

 For the joy of being OUTSIDE, from morning to night.

 To get some fresh air, that of the world and that of the land, that which the morning whips up and the afternoon smothers.

 To advance in the light of day, stripped of the trappings of social life, truly free to go wherever you want and use time as you see fit.

 To put the body to the test. What's the one that life has lent me for nearly fifty years now really worth? It's worth all the effort. I'm infinitely grateful to it for having carried me through to the end.

 And what about Bernard's, which has been doing brilliantly for seventy-six years now? Despite aching feet near the end, he has proven yet again that walking is a darn-good rejuvenating balm. Not only is Bernard the "king of the road," he's a veritable walking machine with unshakable determination. Amazing.

 As pedestrians, we were incredibly vulnerable, but no matter: it's crazy how rooted to the asphalt we felt, as if magnetized by the earth. Try running us over, but we'd keep right on going!

 Another reason: to try and make sense out of this jumble of hatreds and intolerances (we're still working on that). And to store up the thousands of heartfelt smiles, honking horns, and waving hands people sent our way— they'll fuel a grand bonfire that will keep us warm all winter long!

 To make time last rather than constantly compressing it. The universe is endlessly expanding, so why not our miserable—though considerable—lives?

 To (re-)discover a sense of the present, which is none other than that of being alive (now I just need to try not to lose it!), and to imagine the future. I slipped a copy of good old Guyau into my e-reader, and he puts *it better than I could: "You have to desire it, you have to want it; you have to stretch out your hand and walk to create the future. The future is not what comes toward us, but what we travel toward."**

I traveled toward something.

I set out with the following words by Nicolas Bouvier in my head: "Travelling outgrows its motives. It soon proves sufficient in itself. You think you are making a trip, but soon it is making you—or un-making you."†

I don't (yet) know what this journey has made of me. I'll let time answer that. On the other hand, I know what it did not un-make: Bernard and me. Forever.

For those of you who are surprised that we're already home since we were expecting to keep our curtains drawn until the end of November (what did they do, take the train?), a short explanation is in order.

Our roughly prepared walking plan had us arriving in Istanbul on October 26. That would have given us a reasonable window before we'd have to jump back into our work boots and deal with the thousand problems journeys like this one ought to have generated. Well, it turned out to be pointless: no one bothered to steal our passports, no cars ran us over, no bacterium kept us confined to hospital beds. Just a ridiculous case of tendonitis, which twice forced us onto a bus.

Ah, I swear! Long walks ain't what they used to be!

So that's our story. Now we open the house back up, sort through the mail, take care of our wounds, mow the lawn which had a field day, and check on the apples hibernating in the cellar.

All we have left to do is dress the garden soil in a mantle of leaves, beneath which the next burst of life will soon be stirring, then to squeeze the juice from this journey so that it can mature in this year's cask.

---

* Jean-Marie Guyau. *La Genèse de l'idée de temps.* Paris: Félix Alcan, Éditeur, 1890, 33. (*The Origin of the Idea of Time.*)

† Nicolas Bouvier. *The Way of the World.* Marlboro, VT: Marlboro Press, 1992. Translated by Robyn Marsack, 16. French title: *L'usage du monde.* Geneva: Droz, 1963.

*"The virtue of traveling is that it purges life before filling it up."**
Nicolas Bouvier.

BF

---

* Ibid., 27.

EPILOGUE:

THE BALKANS: CORRIDOR BETWEEN LIFE AND DEATH

Journeys home always stir contradictory feelings. We're happy to see our house again, and our friends—but not right away, give us a chance to catch our breath and get over our end-of-the-adventure blues. How strange to wake up two mornings in a row in the same bed. Our minds are a whirl of memories, faces, landscapes. And then there's that inevitable question: *What was it all for?*

Without realizing it in the moment, we sense that something is brewing in the Balkans that will leave a lasting mark on our times. Midway between Syrian or Iraqi violence and peaceful, prosperous Europe, a bidirectional flow, barely visible during our journey, is now, a few months later, quite apparent. Fleeing the war and misery zones—the one giving rise to the other— hundreds of thousands of families have embarked on a mind-boggling migration that, so they thought, would lead them to peace and perhaps even prosperity: to the El Dorados of Germany, Sweden, and Great Britain.

In the other direction, confused teenagers are heading off in search of an absolute that Western society, where consumerism has supplanted the art of living, cannot offer them. Lured by the shiny steel of AK-47s, they abandon their families and friends and make their way to war zones and the deadly fascination of armed conflict.

207

In fact, during our journey, we failed to fully appreciate the scope of this bidirectional flow, of those fleeing death and of those heading off in search of it. Not counting the young people in certain villages who had gone off to wage jihad, and, with our friends Matteo and Cristina in Trieste, those who, at the time, formed but a thin trickle of migrants.

Like Fabrice del Dongo, the naive hero of *The Charterhouse of Parma,*[*] we were smack dab in the middle of a hive of activity, but it was too early, all movement was still underground. Our journey failed to reveal the significance of this developing phenomenon. But it helps us better understand it today.

Who's to blame for this tragic situation? Was it the bungling economists and politicians who pursued globalization for the needs of commerce at all costs and endless economic growth? They claimed to have done away with borders. These miserable, peace-starved migrants took them at their word.

Their odyssey puts our own in perspective. These tens of thousands of men, children, and women with babies in their arms walked in every kind of weather, having packed only a threadbare jacket and a hunk of bread. They, to be sure, are the true champions of the road. Worst of all is having to listen to that handful of well-fed Europeans, awash in scads of possessions from basement to attic, who tremble in their boots before these breadless, shirtless, shoeless souls. What, pray tell, are we afraid of? That they're going to snatch the cake from our mouths? That they're going to run off with a few of the gadgets that clutter our lives and prevent us from thinking?

Let us therefore infuse into our own lives a little of the generosity and fraternity exhibited daily by the poor and the displaced.

---

* TN: *La Chartreuse de Parme* by Stendhal (1839).

ACKNOWLEDGMENTS

I wish to express my gratitude to the staff of the Seuil Association, both paid and unpaid, who kindly kept the organization running while its president of the day was away. Special thanks to our volunteer director Paul Dall'Acqua, and Patrick Beghin, who did an excellent job filling in for the rather irresponsible walking president.

Our appreciation extends to many others as well. Adventures are only possible when those leaving can do so in the knowledge that, at their return, they'll find their nest waiting for them, where they can tend to their wounds and draw lessons from the journey. During our several-months-long absence, a few kind souls not only looked after the day-to-day matters we left behind, but even resolved unforeseen issues that might easily have spoiled our return. Thanks to Thomas and Ariane who handled the emergencies; thanks to Éliane, Christine, and Geneviève who kept an eye on our big house and transformed autumn's beautiful fruits into delicacies we'll savor all winter long, while dreaming of our next journey by the warmth of a crackling fire.

A word of appreciation, finally, to all those who welcomed us into their homes: Giacomo and Ilaria, Jérôme and Güler, Annie and Rico. Your friendship gave us shelter from the storm.

Thanks to Christophe and Agnieszka of the Petit Théâtre Dakoté who waited until Bénédicte was back before kicking off rehearsals for *The Marriage of Figaro*. Thanks, too, to Martine, Marianne, and Françoise for their suggestions and comments on the manuscript.

ABOUT THE AUTHORS

BERNARD OLLIVIER

April 1998. Six days into retirement—still grieving the loss of his wife and his children grown and living on their own—Bernard Ollivier set out to hike the Way of St. James from Paris, France, to Santiago de Compostela, Spain, hoping to figure out a way forward. Fifteen hundred miles later, transformed by the journey, he returned home with two distinct aims. First, having experienced the power of walking for himself, he would figure out a way to help troubled teens get their lives back on track by embarking on accompanied long walks. And second, he would set out on a new long walk, down yet another of history's great roads. In May 1999, he set out on the 7,500-mile Great Silk Road, from Turkey to China. And in the year 2000, he founded the nonprofit Seuil Association, which, working in tandem with French social services, offers young men and women in difficulty an opportunity to avoid prison by embarking on chaperoned long walks in foreign countries.

Since his Silk Road adventure, Ollivier has written several books, both fiction and nonfiction, and, along with his life partner Bénédicte Flatet, has become actively engaged in climate action, in particular through the Air.e Association, which they cofounded. The pair resides in Normandy, in a rustic home surrounded by a veritable forest of trees that Ollivier planted himself.

BÉNÉDICTE FLATET

Bernard Ollivier and Bénédicte Flatet met in August 2008 along the banks of the Loire River. Ollivier, attempting to canoe the river's entire length, had accepted Flatet's offer to put him up for the night.

211

They hit it off and have been together ever since. A graduate of the city of Tours's Conservatoire Francis Poulenc, Flatet is a singer, scriptwriter, actress, and stage director, having performed and directed both in France and internationally, including several years at France's world-famous Avignon Festival. Ollivier's final Silk Road journey, across Europe from France to Turkey, was in fact Flatet's idea; she had long dreamed of accompanying Ollivier on one of his long walks. And so, quite naturally, Ollivier decided to include some of the chronicles Flatet texted back to friends during their journey, making her an author in her own right, and conveying in the narrative that this is truly a *voyage à deux*. In recent years, Flatet has focused her energies on another of her interests: the climate crisis. Her passion for permaculture led the pair to create an impressive organic vegetable garden at the couple's home in Normandy, complete with rain barrels and composting outhouse. And, in 2019, Ollivier and Flatet established the nonprofit Air.e Association, which seeks to promote awareness of planetary ecological collapse and seeking concrete solutions.

SEUIL

Walking, as I've learned myself, has therapeutic benefits: walking helps you grow, walking sets you free, walking will reveal sides of yourself and inner resources you never knew you had.

—Bernard Ollivier

The Seuil Association, founded by Bernard Ollivier, organizes transformative long walks for young men and women struggling to find their place in society. As an alternative to juvenile detention centers or prison, participants commit to walking at least 2,000 kilometers (1,240 miles) in a foreign country, leaving electronic devices behind. In France, over 700 young persons are in prison and 600 in residential treatment centers (Gaëlle de la Brosse, *Le Pèlerin*, July 16, 2020). As of June 2022, Seuil has helped over 323 teens and has an impressive long-term success rate of 76 percent.

Seuil works hand in hand with the French Ministry of Justice's *Protection judiciaire de la jeunesse* (Judicial Protection of Young Persons) program and *Aide sociale à l'enfance* (Child Social Services).

For more information and to donate:
The Seuil Association
31, rue Planchat
75020 Paris
Telephone: +011 33 (0)1 44 27 09 88
Fax: +011 33 (0)1 40 46 01 97
Email: assoseuil@wanadoo.fr
Website: assoseuil.org

AIR.E

The Air.e Association, a grassroots resilience organization founded in 2019 by Bernard Ollivier and Bénédicte Flatet, seeks to build a sustainable world for tomorrow by focusing on local, concrete solutions. Air.e promotes awareness of climate change and impending environmental collapse through organized walks, cultural events, local initiatives, and seminars. Another of Air.e's goals is to create a network of self-sustaining villages where Villagers—*Villag'aires*—can reside and lead fulfilling lives in harmony with nature.

Air.e's first *Marche pour Demain* (Walk for Tomorrow) took place in Brittany in July 2021. Events drew attention to the climate crisis and allowed members interested in Air.e's eco-village project to assemble and develop a collaborative course of action. Future walks are planned for 2022 and beyond.

For further information:
Air.e
Lieu-dit L'Estremeur
29800 Ploudalmezeau FRANCE
Email: contact@air-e.org
Website: https://air-e.org

WALKING AS A
WAY OF LIFE

Go out and walk. That is the glory of life.
                         —Maira Kalman

I picked up the first volume in the *"Longue marche"* series while on a trip to France nearly ten years ago and was instantly hooked: A retiree decides he wants more out of life and starts walking, first from Paris to Santiago de Compostela along the Way of Saint James, then from Turkey to China along the Great Silk Road. I found the idea of dropping everything to go for a walk, almost on a whim, fascinating. And I especially appreciated Ollivier's focus on the people met along the way.

While working on those first three volumes, I had no idea that Bernard Ollivier and his new partner in life Bénédicte Flatet had together completed a fourth leg across Europe, the tale of which was already on French bookshelves. I'm grateful that Skyhorse Publishing picked this volume up too, completing Ollivier's Silk Road journey for English readers.

I met the authors for the first time in the summer of 2019 and spent a few days with Ollivier again in 2023. A warm, soft-spoken man with a cheerful yet pensive spirit, Ollivier is both pragmatic and philosophical. He's an experienced, self-taught journalist. His prose is so detailed and engaging that readers often say they feel as if they're walking right alongside him. He lives in the idyllic Normandy countryside, owns a cat named Lilas, and has planted hundreds of trees on his property. As for Bénédicte, she radiates a passion both for her work in the arts (especially theatre) and for the immense perma-culture garden she and Ollivier have created at their home.

While both quite fit, they are not so different from anyone else. A few pages along in the narrative, it is easy to lose sight of their accomplishment: 560 miles from Lyon, France, to Verona, Italy, then 1,250 miles from Verona to Istanbul, Turkey. Slightly farther than the distance from New York to Denver, covered at an average speed of over twenty miles per day. That is to say, each time you turn a page, they've gone another 8.5 miles.

To better connect with their experience, I broke up long hours of translating by taking walks, typically four or five miles at a time, with a small pack on my back. Ollivier and Flatet, on the other hand, traveled over twenty miles *each day* while towing well over thirty pounds of gear and provisions behind them on a cart. Still, as I dined with Bernard and Bénédicte at their home in 2019, their feat seemed within anyone's reach.

Going the distance, though, is by no means what *Back to Istanbul* is all about. Ollivier and Flatet give thought to many issues as they walk. They reflect on relationships, on the unexpected abilities we all possess, on what it means to grow old, and on how we are often capable of more than we realize. Ollivier set out from Istanbul in 1999 at the age of sixty-two and reached Xi'an at sixty-six. In this volume, he starts out at seventy-five, with the youthful, forty-seven-year-old Bénédicte by his side. In the West, though retirement can bring a degree of personal freedom, the pair lament how seniors are seldom fully integrated into society: the wealth of knowledge they possess is rarely tapped by those busy with gainful employment.

While walking changes the way one sees the world, the world also deals differently with foot travelers. A great equalizer, walking effaces social class differences and fosters encounters. Tourists are no longer observers but participants. On foot, we more easily connect with others, whereas in a plane, bus, or car, conversation is often impossible or at best superficial. Walking encounters are therefore more meaningful. It is also a metaphor: as we walk with others, we leave the familiar behind and embrace the unknown.

In those encounters, familiarity with local languages is a handy skill, as it allows for more extended conversations. Ollivier and Flatet, though—who, except for Italian, speak none of the languages along their route—are obliged to do their best by employing abundant hand gestures and broad smiles whenever their phrasebooks fail them.

Walking connects us with places as well, for "Is there any better way to immerse yourself in a country than to walk across it, step by step?" Through Flatet and Ollivier's journey, readers discover the Balkans: countries with which many citizens of the US, at least, remain unfamiliar.

Despite Europe's incredibly beautiful scenery, as Ollivier and Flatet slowly make their way across the continent, they cannot help but notice environmental degradation: urban sprawl, endless lines of motor vehicles, pollution. How can one see the world as it is and not feel compelled to sound the alarm? Ollivier and Flatet's experience has turned them into partisans of degrowth and full-fledged environmentalists: in 2020, they founded the Air.e Association, which seeks to draw attention to a planet in crisis and develop solutions.

Motorized travel contributes to ecological breakdown. Though they hail from a country of high-speed TGV trains, Ollivier and Flatet advocate slow, environmentally friendly modes of transportation, that age-old and most sustainable one above all: walking. Walking is freedom: freedom from the limitations and harmful effects of mechanized travel.

Through connections with people and places, through slowness and introspection, the ultimate focus of Ollivier and Flatet's narrative is on healing: on healing the self and the planet; on rebirth.

While most of us may not walk as far as they do, we can nevertheless be inspired by their endeavor. By introducing short walks into our lives, by prioritizing slow forms of travel that allow us to mingle with locals, by practicing travel minimalism, or by simply sharing back home what we learn from those encountered, we can not only avoid impacting those people and places negatively, we can actually help them.

For their good counsel, I would like to thank Dr. Jennifer Wolter, professor at Ohio's Bowling Green State University, and my editor, Jon Arlan. Any remaining weaknesses in this translation are my own. I'm deeply grateful to the National Endowment for the Arts and especially to the NEA's 2017 translation fellowship evaluation committee for sensing the importance of the *Longue marche* series. Lastly, thoughts of my dear high school French teacher, Darlene Hindsley, were often with me as I worked.

And with that, I believe it's time for me to go for a walk.

—*Dan Golembeski*